A BEGINNERS' GUIDE TO 2D PLATFORM GAMES WITH UNITY

Create a simple 2D platform game and learn to code in the process

Patrick Felicia

A Beginner's Guide to

2D Platform Games

with Unity

First published: December 2016

Published by Patrick Felicia

CREDITS

Author: Patrick Felicia

ABOUT THE AUTHOR

Patrick Felicia is a <u>lecturer and researcher</u> at Waterford Institute of Technology, where he teaches and supervises undergraduate and postgraduate students. He obtained his MSc in Multimedia Technology in 2003 and PhD in Computer Science in 2009 from University College Cork, Ireland. He has published several books and articles on the use of video games for educational purposes, including the Handbook of Research on Improving Learning and Motivation through Educational Games: Multidisciplinary Approaches (published by IGI), and Digital Games in Schools: a Handbook for Teachers, published by European Schoolnet. Patrick is also the Editor-in-chief of the <u>International Journal of Game-Based Learning (IJGBL),</u> and the Conference Director of the <u>Irish Conference on Game-Based Learning</u>, a popular conference on games and learning organized throughout Ireland.

SUPPORT AND RESOURCES FOR THIS BOOK

To complete the activities presented in this book you need to download the start-up pack on the companion website; it consists of free resources that you will need to complete your projects, including bonus material that will help you along the way (e.g., cheat sheets, introductory videos, code samples, and much more).

- Please open the following link:

http://learntocreategames.com/2d-platform-games/

- In the section called "**Download your Free Resource Pack**", enter your email address and your first name, and click on the button labeled "**Yes, I want to receive my bonus pack**".

- After a few seconds, you should receive a link to your free start-up pack.

- When you receive the link, you can download all the resources to your computer.

This book is dedicated to Helena

TABLE OF CONTENTS

PREFACE

After teaching Unity for over 5 years, I always thought it could be great to find a book that could get my students started with Unity in a few hours and that showed them how to master the core functionalities offered by this fantastic software.

Many of the books that I found were too short and did not provide enough details on the why behind the actions recommended and taken; other books were highly theoretical, and I found that they lacked practicality and that they would not get my students' full attention. In addition, I often found that game development may be preferred by those with a programming background but that those with an Arts background, even if they wanted to get to know how to create games, often had to face the issue of learning to code for the first time.

As a result, I started to consider a format that would cover both: be approachable (even to the students with no programming background), keep students highly motivated and involved using an interesting project, cover the core functionalities available in Unity to get started with game programming, provide answers to common questions, and also provide, if need be, a considerable amount of details for some topics.

I then created a book series entitled **Unity From Zero to Proficiency** that did just this. It gave readers the opportunity to play around with Unity's core features, and essentially those that will make it possible to create an interesting 3D game rapidly. After reading this book series, many readers emailed me to let me know how the book series helped them; however, they also mentioned that what they also wanted was to be able to create a simple game from start to finish, publish it and share it with their friends, or learn more about other features such as Artificial Intelligence, Animations, or Shaders.

This is the reason why I created this new book series entitled "**A Beginner's Guide**"; it is for people who already have completed the first four books in the series called **Unity From Zero to Proficiency**, and who would like to focus on a particular aspect of their game development. This being said, this new book series assumes no prior knowledge on the part of the reader, and it will get you started quickly on a particular aspect of Unity.

In this book, focused on 2D platformers, you will be completing a 2D platformer game and also code in C#. By completing each chapter, and by following step-by-step instructions, you will progressively create a complete 2D platformer game.

You will also create a 2D game that includes many of the common techniques found in platformers, including: level design, object creation, moving platforms, magic doors, simple artificial intelligence, and a user interface.

CONTENT COVERED BY THIS BOOK

- *Chapter 1, Creating a Simple Level,* shows you how to create a simple level for a platformer game, including a main character, platforms, cameras following the player, and sprites that you can collect or avoid.

- *Chapter 2, Managing Score, Lives and Levels,* explains how it is possible to manage the score and the number of lives across your scenes; you will also learn how to load a new scene based on conditions, and to also minimize your development time by using prefabs.

- *Chapter 3, Adding Sound and Displaying Values Onscreen,* explains how you can simply add audio to your game, and display or update information onscreen (e.g., number of lives or score).

- *Chapter 4, Adding Challenging Gameplay,* shows and explains how to make your platform game more challenging by adding common game mechanics (e.g., platforms, magic doors, escalator, etc.).

- *Chapter 5* provides answers to Frequently Asked Questions (FAQs) related to the topics covered in this book.

- *Chapter 6* summarizes the topics covered in the book and provides you with more information on the next steps to follow.

WHAT YOU NEED TO USE THIS BOOK

To complete the project presented in this book, you only need Unity 5.0 (or a more recent version) and to also ensure that your computer and its operating system comply with Unity's requirements. Unity can be downloaded from the official website (http://www.unity3d.com/download), and before downloading it, you can check that your computer is up to scratch on the following page: http://www.unity3d.com/unity/system-requirements. At the time of writing this book, the following operating systems are supported by Unity for development: Windows XP (i.e., SP2+, 7 SP1+), Windows 8, and Mac OS X 10.6+. In terms of graphics card, most cards produced after 2004 should be suitable.

In terms of computer skills, all knowledge introduced in this book will assume no prior programming experience from the reader. So for now, you only need to be able to perform common computer tasks, such as downloading items, opening and saving files, be comfortable with dragging and dropping items and typing, and be relatively comfortable with Unity's interface. This being said, because the focus of this book is on creating 2D platform games, and while all instructions are explained step-by-step, you may need to be relatively comfortable with Unity's interface, and coding in C#, as well as creating and transforming objects (e.g., moving, or rotating).

So, if you would prefer to become more comfortable with Unity and C# programming prior to starting this book, you can download the books in the series called Unity 5 From Zero to Proficiency (Foundations, Beginner, Intermediate, or Advanced). These books cover most of the shortcuts and views available in Unity, as well as how to perform common tasks in Unity, such as creating objects, transforming objects, importing assets, using navigation controllers, creating scripts or exporting the game to the web. They also explain how to code your game using both UnityScript or C# along with good coding practices.

WHO THIS BOOK IS FOR

If you can answer **yes** to all these questions, then this book is for you:

1. Would you like to learn how to create a 2D platformer?

2. Would you like to know how to create reusable objects and save yourself some time?

3. Can you already code in C#?

4. Would you like to discover how to create a menu and levels?

5. Although you may have had some prior exposure to Unity and coding, would you like to delve more into 2D platformer games?

WHO THIS BOOK IS NOT FOR

If you can answer yes to all these questions, then this book is **not** for you:

1. Can you already create 2D platformers?

2. Can you create menus and levels for 2D games?

3. Are you looking for a reference book on Unity programming?

4. Are you an experienced (or at least advanced) Unity user?

If you can answer yes to all four questions, you may instead look for the next book in the series on the official website.

HOW YOU WILL LEARN FROM THIS BOOK

Because all students learn differently and have different expectations of a course, this book is designed to ensure that all readers find a learning mode that suits them. Therefore, it includes the following:

- A list of the learning objectives at the start of each chapter so that readers have a snapshot of the skills that will be covered.

- Each section includes an overview of the activities covered.

- Many of the activities are step-by-step, and learners are also given the opportunity to engage in deeper learning and problem-solving skills through the challenges offered at the end of each chapter.

- Each chapter ends-up with a quiz and challenges through which you can put your skills (and knowledge acquired) into practice, and see how much you know. Challenges consist in coding, debugging, or creating new features based on the knowledge that you have acquired in the chapter.

- The book focuses on the core skills that you need; some sections also go into more detail; however, once concepts have been explained, links are provided to additional resources, where necessary.

- The code is introduced progressively and is explained in detail.

- You also gain access to several videos that help you along the way, especially for the most challenging topics.

FORMAT OF EACH CHAPTER AND WRITING CONVENTIONS

Throughout this book, and to make reading and learning easier, text formatting and icons will be used to highlight parts of the information provided and to make it more readable.

The full solution for the project presented in this book is available for download on the official website (http://learntocreategames.com/2d-platform-games/).

SPECIAL NOTES

Each chapter includes resource sections, so that you can further your understanding and mastery of Unity; these include:

- A quiz for each chapter: these quizzes usually include 10 questions that test your knowledge of the topics covered throughout the chapter. The solutions are provided on the companion website.

- A checklist: it consists of between 5 and 10 key concepts and skills that you need to be comfortable with before progressing to the next chapter.

- Challenges: each chapter includes a challenge section where you are asked to combine your skills to solve a particular problem.

Author's notes appear as described below:

> Author's suggestions appear in this box.

Code appears as described below:

```
public int score;
public string playersName = "Sam";
```

Checklists that include the important points covered in the chapter appear as described below:

- Item1 for check list

- Item2 for check list

- Item3 for check list

HOW CAN YOU LEARN BEST FROM THIS BOOK

- **Talk to your friends about what you are doing.**

  We often think that we understand a topic until we have to explain it to friends and answer their questions. By explaining your different projects, what you just learned will become clearer to you.

- **Do the exercises.**

  All chapters include exercises that will help you to learn by doing. In other words, by completing these exercises, you will be able to better understand the topic and gain practical skills (i.e., rather than just reading).

- **Don't be afraid of making mistakes.**

  I usually tell my students that making mistakes is part of the learning process; the more mistakes you make and the more opportunities you have for learning. At the start, you may find the errors disconcerting, or that the engine does not work as expected until you understand what went wrong.

- **Export your games early.**

  It is always great to build and export your first game. Even if it is rather simple, it is always good to see it in a browser and to be able to share it with you friends.

- **Learn in chunks.**

  It may be disconcerting to go through five or six chapters straight, as it may lower your motivation. Instead, give yourself enough time to learn, go at your own pace, and learn in small units (e.g., between 15 and 20 minutes per day). This will do at least two things for you: it will give your brain the time to "digest" the information that you have just learned, so that you can start fresh the following day. It will also make sure that you don't "burn-out" and that you keep your motivation levels high.

FEEDBACK

While I have done everything possible to produce a book of high quality and value, I always appreciate feedback from readers so that the book can be improved accordingly. If you would like to give feedback, you can email me at learntocreategames@gmail.com.

DOWNLOADING THE SOLUTIONS FOR THE BOOK

You can download the solutions for this book after creating a free online account at http://learntocreategames.com/2d-platform-games/. Once you have registered, a link to the files will be sent to you automatically.

IMPROVING THE BOOK

Although great care was taken in checking the content of this book, I am human, and some errors could remain in the book. As a result, it would be great if you could let me know of any issue or error you may have come across in this book, so that it can be solved and the book updated accordingly. To report an error, you can email me (learntocreategames@gmail.com) with the following information:

- Name of the book.

- The page or section where the error was detected.

- Describe the error and also what you think the correction should be.

Once your email is received, the error will be checked, and, in the case of a valid error, it will be corrected and the book page will be updated to reflect the changes accordingly.

SUPPORTING THE AUTHOR

A lot of work has gone into this book and it is the fruit of long hours of preparation, brainstorming, and finally writing. As a result, I would ask that you do not distribute any illegal copies of this book.

This means that if a friend wants a copy of this book, s/he will have to buy it through the official channels (i.e., through Amazon, lulu.com, or the book's official website: www.learntocreategames.com/learn-unity-ebook).

If some of your friends are interested in the book, you can refer them to the book's official website (http://www.learntocreategames.com/learn-unity-ebook) where they can either buy the book, enter a monthly draw to be in for a chance of receiving a free copy of the book, or to be notified of future promotional offers.

1
CREATING A SIMPLE LEVEL

In this section, we will start by creating a simple level, including:

- A 2D character that will be able to jump and walk.

- Simple platforms.

- A camera that follows the player.

- A mini-map that displays the layout of the level.

- Objects that you can collect.

- Objects that bounce indefinitely.

So, after completing this chapter, you will be able to:

- Use a character that can jump and walk.

- Create 2D objects.

- Create a C# script.

- Detect collisions between objects.

- Destroy objects upon collision.

[17]

INTRODUCTION

In this chapter we will create a simple level with a 2D character that can walk and bounce off platforms; we will also create objects that the character has to collect or to avoid, and some of them will also have physics properties, which will make it possible for them to bounce.

ADDING THE MAIN CHARACTER

The very first thing that we will do is to create a simple 2D scene that includes a 2D character along with several platforms.

Luckily, Unity includes a set of 2D assets that we can use for this purpose. So we will proceed as follows:

- Import the 2D assets (including a 2D character).

- Create platforms from basic shapes (i.e., boxes).

- Create a camera that follows the main character.

- Create a mini-map.

So let's get started:

- Please launch Unity.

- Create a new project (**File | New Project**).

- Once the new project is open, please select the **2D** mode for the scene, by clicking on the 2D button located in the top left corner of the **Scene** view.

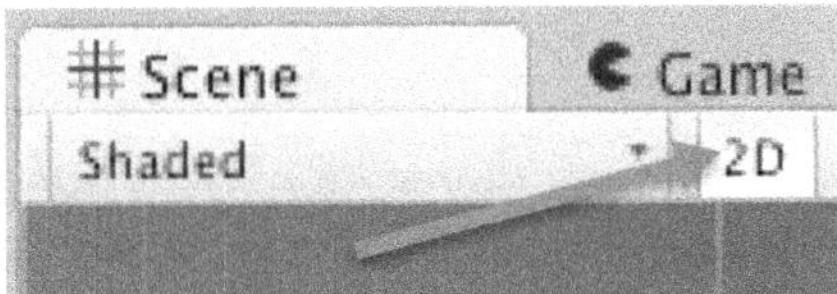

Figure 1: Using the 2D mode

Next, we will import some of the necessary assets to create our scene.

- Please select: **Assets | Import Package | 2D** from the top menu.

- A new window called **Import Unity Package** will appear.

- Please click on the button called **Import** to import all **2D** assets.

- This will create a new folder called **Standard Assets** in the **Project** window, and within this folder, another folder called **2D** which includes several **2D** assets that we will use.

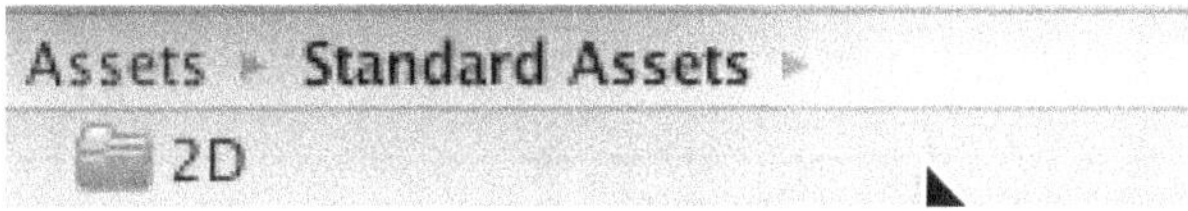

Figure 2: The new folder for 2D assets

Once this is done, it is time to add our 2D character:

- In the **Project** window, from the folder **Standard Assets | 2D | Prefabs**, drag and drop the prefab called **CharacterRobotBoy** to the **Scene** view (if you don't feel comfortable with navigating through the different views and window in Unity, you may consider reading the book **Unity from Zero to proficiency - Foundations**).

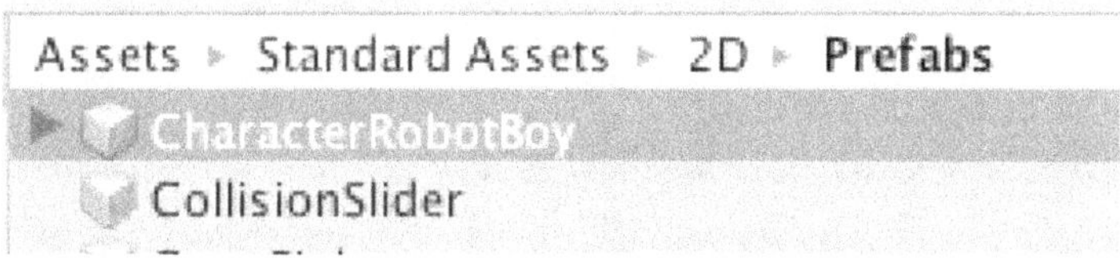

Figure 3: Adding the character

As you will see, this will create a new object called **CharacterRobotBoy** in the **Hierarchy** view. It will also add a character to the scene, as illustrated on the next figure.

Figure 4: The game object CharacterRobotBoy

- You can set the position of this character to **(0, 2, 0)** using the **Inspector**.

> Note that if your background does not look like the one illustrated on the previous figure, it is probably because a background image was not added automatically by Unity; you can change the background of your scene using the window: **Window | Lightings**.

- If you click on this character in the **Scene** view, and then look at the **Inspector**, you should see that it includes several components, including a **Sprite Renderer** (to display the character), an **Animator** component (for the walking or jumping animations), two colliders (circle and box colliders), a **Rigidbody2D** component (so that it is subject to forces, including gravity) along with two scripts used to control the character. We don't need to know the content of the scripts for now; however, it is always good to have an idea of the different necessary component for this character.

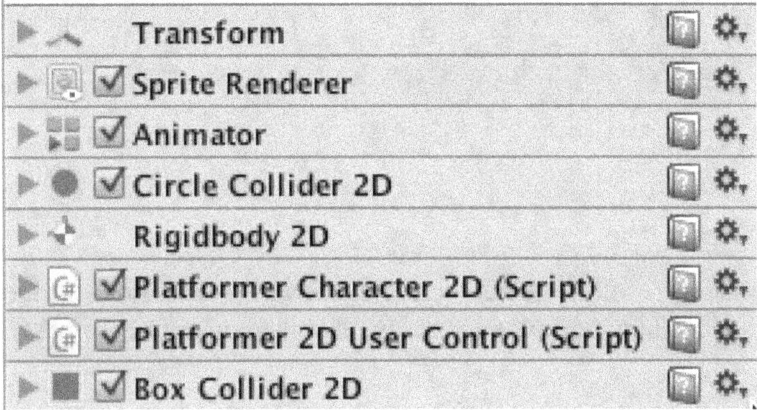

Figure 5: Components for the RobotBoy character

Once this is done, you can play the scene, and you will see that the character will fall indefinitely; this is because of its **Rigidbody** component which exerts gravity on this character and also due to the fact that there is no ground or platform under the character; so the next thing we will do is to create a simple platform on which the player can walk.

> Note that to play and stop the scene, you can press the shortcut CTRL + P, or use the black triangle located at the top of the window.
>
> 

- Please create a new box: from the **Project** window, select **Create | Sprites | Square**.

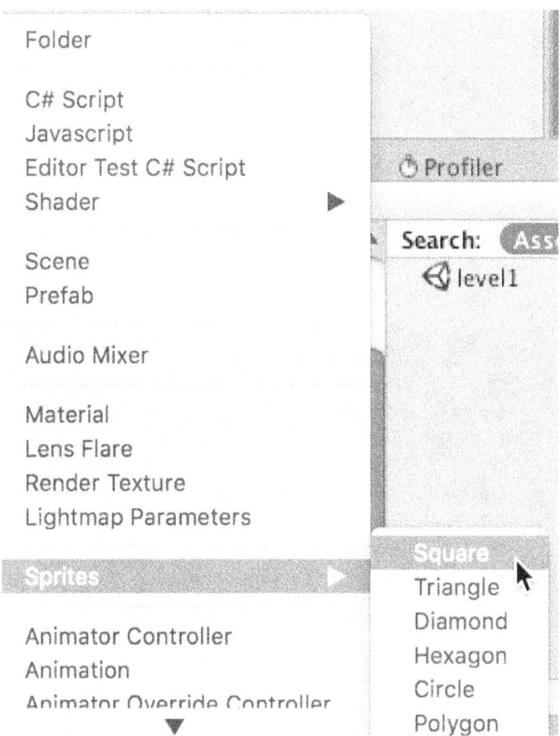

Figure 6: Creating a new sprite (square) – part 1

- This will create a **Sprite** asset;

- Please rename it **platform**.

Note that because this is an asset, it will be accessible throughout the project, irrespective of the scene that is open.

Figure 7: Creating a new sprite (square) – part 2

Once this is done, you can drag and drop this asset (i.e., the platform) to the **Scene** view.

- This will create a new object called **platform**.

- You can then resize this object, so that it looks like a platform, and place it just below the character; for example, you could set its scale property to **(18, 1, 1)** and its position to **(-6, -1.5, 0)**.

Figure 8: Adding a platform

Next, we need to add a collider to this object so that the player effectively collides with it (and stops falling).

- Please select the object called **platform** (i.e., the object that you have just created).

- From the top menu, select **Component | Physics2D | BoxCollider2D**.

- This will add a **2DCollider** (shaped as a box) to our **platform** object.

- You can then duplicate this platform and move the duplicate to its right; you may also change the **scale** attribute of the duplicate to **(33, 1, 1)** so that your scene looks like the following figure.

Figure 9: The character and two platforms

Note that you can, if you wish, modify the color of each platform by selecting (and modifying) the attribute called **color** that is accessible within the component called **Sprite Renderer** for each platform.

You can now test the scene; you can move the character using the **arrow keys** (to go left and right), the **space bar** (to jump), or the **CTRL** key (to crouch).

FOLLOWING THE PLAYER WITH CAMERAS

Perfect. So we have a character that can move around the scene and jump on platforms; the only thing is that, whenever this character is outside the screen, we can't see it anymore; so we will need to make sure that it is onscreen all the time; and this can be achieved by setting the main camera to follow this character. Luckily, as part of the 2D assets, Unity provides a simple script, that can be applied to any camera, so that it follows a specific target. So we will use this script on the main camera so that it follows the character.

So let's do the following:

- In the **Hierarchy** window, please select the object called **MainCamera**.

- Then, after locating the folder **Standard Assets | 2D | Scripts** in the **Project** view, drag and drop the script called **Camera2DFollow** from this folder to the object called **MainCamera** in the **Hierarchy** window.

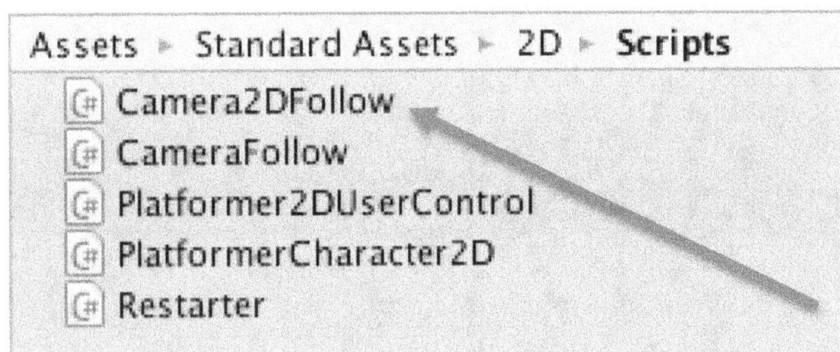

Figure 10: Adding the Camera2DFollow script

- Once this is done, please select the object called **MainCamera** in the **Hierarchy** window.

- As you do so, you will see, in the **Inspector** window, that it includes a new component, which is our script, and that this component also includes an empty field called **target**; this field will be used to specify the target for this camera (in our case, this will be the object **CharcaterRobotBoy**).

Figure 11: Setting the target for the camera (part 1)

- Please drag and drop the object called **CharacerRobotBoy** from the **Hierarchy** window to this field (to the right of the label **Target**).

Figure 12: Setting the target for the camera (part 2)

- Once this is done, please test the scene, and check that the camera is now focusing on your character.

Figure 13: Following the character with the camera

CREATING A MINI-MAP

OK, so now our character is in focus and we can move it around the scene; however, wouldn't it be great to be able to see the overall scene (or what's ahead of the character) in the form of a mini-map; we could create a map displayed in the top right-corner of the window that shows a global view of the level; so let's do just that.

- Please create a new camera (**GameObject | Camera**) and rename it **mini-map**.

- Using the **Inspector**, change its **z** position value to **-20** (this is its depth and it indicates how close/far the camera will be from the player).

- Using the **Inspector,** change its **Viewport Rect** options to: **X = .75, Y= .75, W=.25, H=.25,** and **depth =1**.

> The **ViewportRect** defines where the image captured by the camera is displayed; all these parameters are expressed as a proportion of the screen and range from 0 to 1. So in our case the top-left corner of this view port is located at 75% of the screen's height and 75% of the screen's width (i.e., **X = .75 and Y = .75**); its width is 25% of the screen's width and its height is 25% of the screen's height.

- Please add (i.e., drag and drop) the **2DCameraFollow** script (from the folder **Standard Assets | 2D | Scripts**) to the new camera (i.e., **mini-map**).

- Using the **Inspector**, set the target of the camera to the **CharacterRobotBoy** object, as we have done previously for the other camera: drag and drop the object called **CharacerRobotBoy** from the **Hierarchy** window to the field called **target** for this script.

Figure 14: Setting the target for the second camera

- Please test the scene, and you should see an overview of the level in the top-right corner of the screen.

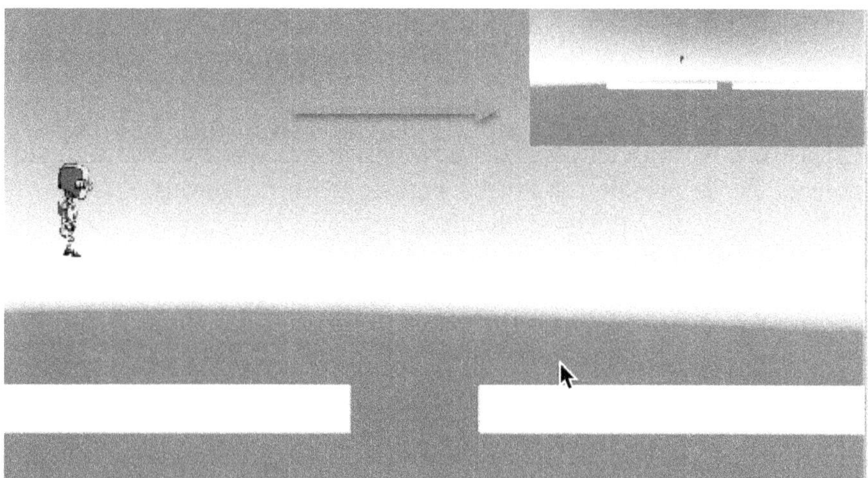

Figure 15: Displaying the mini-map

ADDING OBJECTS TO COLLECT

In this section, we will learn how to detect collisions; this will be used for our character to be able to collect objects, but to also detect when it collides with dangerous objects.

The process will be as follows, we will:

- Create new sprites that will be used as objects to collect or avoid.

- Create and apply tags to these objects (i.e., labels).

- Create a script, linked to the player, that will detect collisions and that will also detect the tag of the object we are colliding with.

- Depending on the tag of this object, we will trigger different actions (e.g., restart the current level or increase the score).

So let's get started.

- Please create a new circular sprite: from the Project window, select: **Create | Sprites | Circle**.

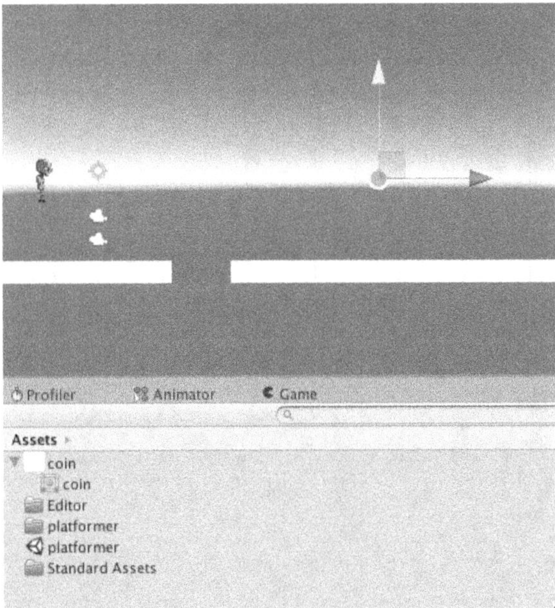

Figure 16: Creating a new sprite for coins

- In the **Project** window, rename this object **coin** (i.e., right-click + select the option **Rename**), and drag and drop it to the **Scene** view; this will create an object called **coin**.

- Zoom-in on the coin: select **SHIFT + F**.

- Using the **Inspector**, we can change its color to yellow (i.e., using the color attribute for the component **Sprite Renderer**).

- You may also ensure that its **z** coordinate is **0**.

We will also need to add a collider to this object (i.e., the coin), so that the player can collide with (and eventually collect) this object:

- Please select the object called **coin** in the **Hierarchy** window; then, using the top menu, select **Component | Physics2D | Circle Collider 2D**. This will create a collider for our coin, so that collisions between the player and this object can be detected.

We can now create the mechanisms to collect the coin; it will consist of a script that will detect collisions between the player and the objects, and, in the case of a collision with a coin, remove or destroy the coin.

First, we will create what is called a **tag**; it will help to identify each object in the scene, and to see what object the player is colliding with.

- Please select the object called **coin** in the Hierarchy.

- In the **Inspector** window, select the option **Add Tag...**

Figure 17: Adding a tag (part 1)

- In the new window, click on the + button and then specify a name for your tag (i.e., **pick_me**), using the field to the right of the label **Tag 0**.

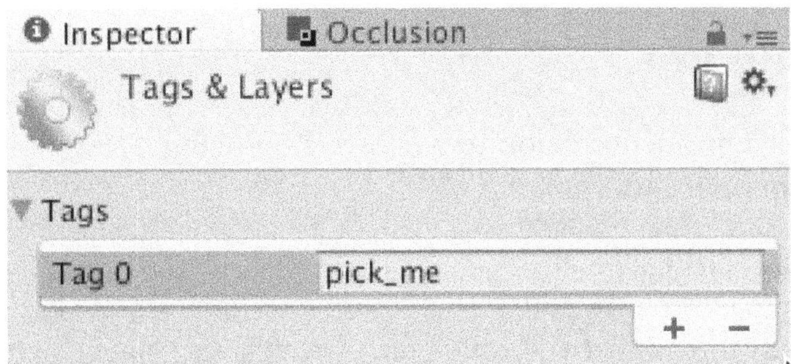

Figure 18: Adding a tag (part 2)

- Press **Return** on your keyboard to save your new tag.

- Select the object **coin** in the **Hierarchy** again, and, using the **Inspector**, select the tag **pick_me**, that you have just created.

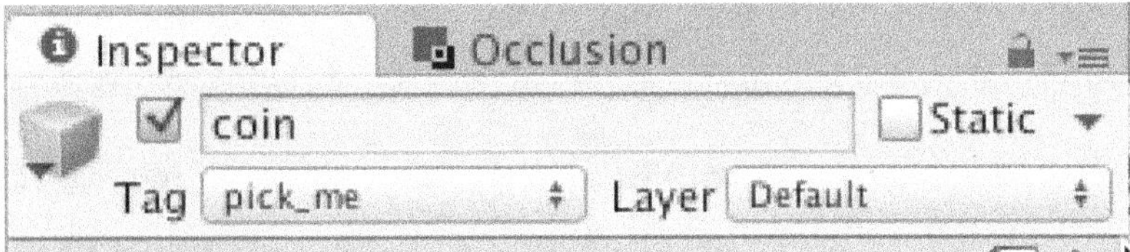

Figure 19: Adding a tag (part 3)

Once the tag has been created, we can now create our new script and detect whether we have collided with an object tagged as **pick_me**.

Creating the collision script

- Please create a new script called **DetectCollision** (i.e., select **Create | C#** from the **Project** window)

- Open this script by double-clicking on it in the **Project** view.

- Add the following code (new code in bold) to this script.

```
using UnityEngine;
public class DetectCollision : MonoBehaviour
{
     void Start () { }
     void Update () {}
     void OnCollisionEnter2D (Collision2D coll)
     {
          string tag = coll.collider.gameObject.tag;
          if (tag == "pick_me")
          {
               Destroy(coll.collider.gameObject);
          }
     }
}
```

In the previous code:

- We declare a function called **OnCollisionEnter2D**.

- This function is called by Unity whenever a collision occurs with the object linked to this script.

Please note that the name of this function is **case-sensitive** which means that when a collision occurs, Unity will call a function called **OnCollisionEnter2D**; however, if you name your function with a different spelling or case, let's say **_on_CollisionEnter2D**, this function will not be called upon collision; so it is important that you use this exact spelling. Interestingly, if you make a spelling mistake, it will still compile, as Unity will assume that you have created your own custom function.

- When a collision occurs and that this function has been defined properly, Unity provides an object of type **Collision2D** that includes information about the collision; we have named this object **coll** here, but any other name could have been used instead.

- We then check the tag of the object that we have collided with using the following code:

```
coll.collider.object.tag;
```

- If the tag is **pick_me**, we then destroy the other object using the following code:

```
Destroy(coll.collider.gameObject);
```

- Once this is done, please save your script, and check that it is error-free.

- Drag and drop this script (**DetectCollision**) on the object **CharacterRobotBoy**.

- Test the scene by moving the character so that it collides with the coin that should now disappear.

ADDING OBSTACLES

Ok, so now that we have created coins to collect, we could also create objects to avoid; in our case, we will code the game, for the time-being, so that colliding with these objects (i.e., the object to be avoided) will cause the player to restart the level.

- Using the **Hierarchy** window, please duplicate the object called **coin**, and rename the duplicate **boulder**. To duplicate this object, you can right-click on it, and select **Rename** from the contextual menu, or select the object and use the shortcut **CTRL + D**.

- Move this object (**boulder**) to the right of the **coin**.

- Change the label of the object called **boulder** to **avoid_me**, by creating (and applying) a new tag called **avoid_me** to it, as we have done in the previous section.

- We will also change its color to **red** using the **Inspector**.

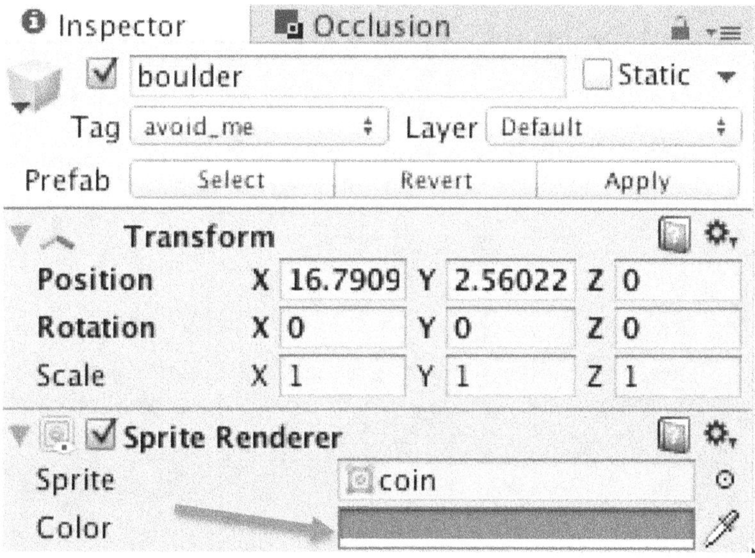

Figure 20: Changing the properties of the boulder

Next, we will add some physics properties to this object so that it bounces on the ground.

ADDING PHYSICS PROPERTIES

- Please select the object called **boulder** in the **Hierarchy**.

- Then, from the top menu, select **Component | Physics2D | Rigidbody2D**; this will create a **Rigidbody2D** component for the **boulder** object, which will now be subject to forces (e.g., gravity or push from the player).

- In the **Project** window, navigate to the folder **Assets | Standard Assets | 2D | Physics Material** and drag and drop the asset called **Bouncy Box** to the object called **boulder**.

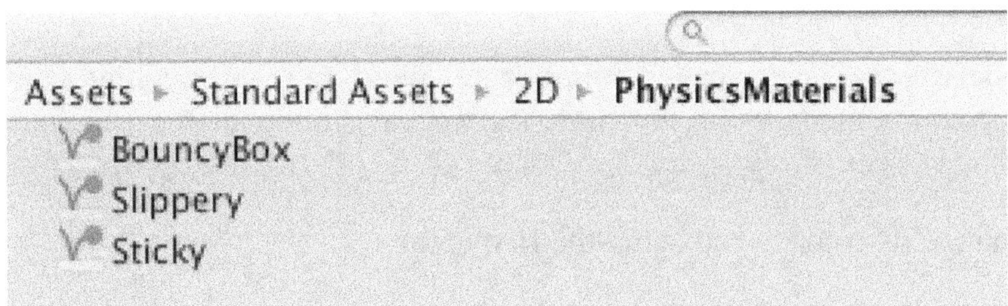

Figure 21: Adding a Physics Material component (part 1)

This will change the **Material** attribute of the **Circle Collider** for this object to **Bouncy Box**.

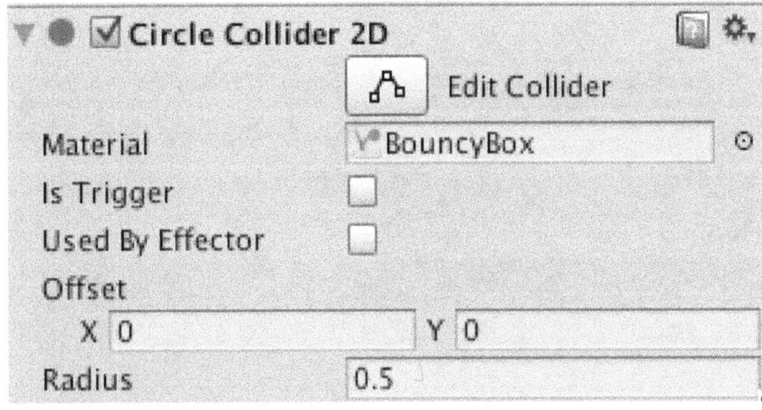

Figure 22: Adding a Physics Material component (part 2)

You can now test the scene, and you should see that the boulder is bouncing; however, it is not bouncing for long; this is because the **Physics** material that we have applied includes some frictions to the boulder; this means that the bouncing will eventually stop as the energy of the ball is progressively absorbed (or dissipated). You can see this by selecting the Physics Material **Bouncy Box** in the folder **Assets| Standard Assets|2D|Physics Material** and by looking at the **Inspector** window.

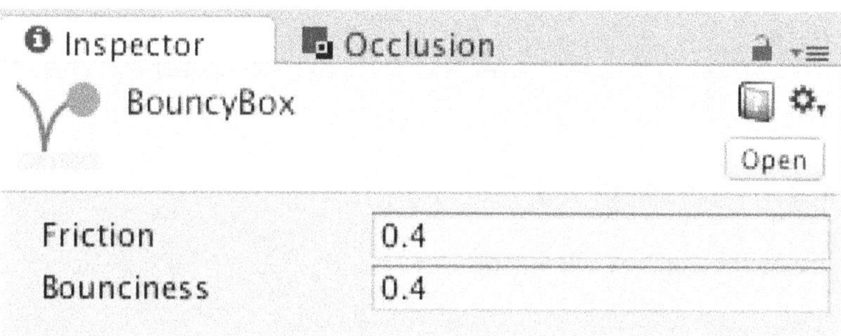

Figure 23: Checking the attributes of the BouncyBox material

As illustrated on the previous figure, we can see that frictions are applied to the boulder when we use this **Physics Material**; so what we will do is to create our own **Physics Material**, and set it up so that no frictions are applied.

- Using the **Project** window, duplicate the material called **Bouncy Box** that is currently in the folder **Assets | Standard Assets | 2D | Physics Material** (left-click on the material to select it, then press *CTRL + D*).

- Rename the duplicate: **MyBouncyBox**.

- Select this new Physics Material (i.e., **MyBouncyBox**) by clicking once on it.

- Using the **Inspector**, change both its **Friction** and **Bounciness** to **1**.

- Last but not least, please drag and drop this new material (i.e., **MyBouncyBox**) on the object **boulder** that is in the **Scene** view, so that this new material is applied instead of the previous one.

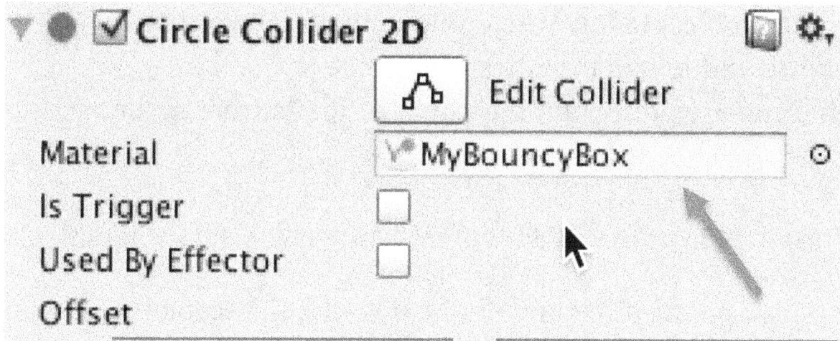

Figure 24: Applying our new Physics Material

- You can now test the game again and see that the boulder is bouncing indefinitely.

RESTARTING THE LEVEL

Once this is done, we just need to modify our collision script so that we restart the current level if we collide with the red boulder.

- Please open the script **DetectCollision** and modify the code as follows.

- Add the following code at the start of the script:

```
using System.Collections;
using UnityEngine.SceneManagement;
```

In the previous code, we add the path to the class called **SceneManagement**; this is because, in the next code, we will be using this class to reload the current scene.

- Add the next code within the method **OnCollisionEnter2D** (new code in bold).

```
if (tag == "pick_me")
{
      Destroy(coll.collider.gameObject);
}
if (tag == "avoid_me")
{

      Destroy(coll.collider.gameObject);
      SceneManager.LoadScene(SceneManager.GetActiveScene().name);

}
```

In the previous code:

- We check that the tag of the object that we are colliding with is **avoid_me**.
- We then destroy this object and reload the current scene.
- We use the class **SceneManager** to obtain the name of the current scene, and to load it.

Once this is done, please save your script, check that it is error-free, and run the game.

Please test the game and check that, upon collision with the boulder, the scene is restarted accordingly.

LEVEL ROUNDUP

In this chapter, we have learnt how to create a simple level with platforms, a main character, and objects that need to be collected or avoided. We also managed to create a camera that follows the player, and a mini-map, along with a script that detects the tags applied to some of the objects in the scene. Finally, we also learned to apply physics materials so that some of the objects (the boulder), could bounce indefinitely. So, we have covered considerable ground to get you started with the first level of your platformer.

Checklist

You can consider moving to the next stage if you can do the following:

- Know how to import the **2D Asset** package.

- Import the asset **CharaterRobotBoy**.

- Use built-in scripts so that a camera can follow a particular target.

- Apply a tag to an object.

- Detect collision from a script.

- Detect the name of a tag from a script.

Quiz

Now, let's check your knowledge! Please answer the following questions (the answers are included in the resource pack) or specify if these statements are either correct or incorrect.

1. The method **OnCollisonEnter2D** is used when a collision has been detected between two sprites.

2. The script **Camera2DFollow**, can be used so that a camera follows a target.

3. Physics materials can be used to paint a sprite.

4. A **View Port** can be used to specify where a camera can be added to the scene.

5. The following code opens the scene called **level1**.

```
Scenemanager.OpenScene("level1");
```

6. Only one camera at a time can be used for a scene.

7. When specifying a viewport for a camera, the values usually range between 0 and 100.

8. It is possible to change the color of a sprite using the component **Sprite Render**.

9. A new sprite can be created using the **Create** menu available in the **Project** view.

10. Only square sprites can be created in Unity.

Challenge 1

Now that you have managed to complete this chapter and that you have created your first level, you could improve the level by doing the following:

- Create additional platforms (e.g., using duplication).

- Change their colors.

- Create other objects to collect with other shapes (e.g., triangle or square) and apply the tag **pick_me** to them.

- Create additional physics materials and apply them to new objects that need to be avoided.

2

MANAGING SCORE, LIVES AND LEVELS

In this section, we will learn how to create and keep track of the score, and the player's number of lives. We will also get to use specific conditions to load a new level.

After completing this chapter, you will be able to:

- Understand the importance of (and use) prefabs.

- Create variables to track the score and the number of lives.

- Understand how to load a new level.

- Create buttons and manage events (i.e., users'clicks).

- Create a simple splash-screen.

INTRODUCTION

In this chapter we will learn how to maximize your time and avoid repeating yourself by using prefabs, which are extremely useful once you start adding them to your games. We will also get to keep track of the score and the number of lives, and complete the structure of our game by creating a **splash-screen** (displayed at the start of the game), a **win** screen (displayed when the player has won) and an **end** screen (displayed when the player has lost).

ADDING AND MANAGING THE SCORE

At present, we can pick-up objects, and it would be great to be able to add a scoring feature, whereby our score is increased by **1** every time we collect a coin.

So let's just add this feature:

- Please open the script **DetectCollision**.

- Add a declaration for a variable **score** as follows (new code in bold):

```
public class DetectCollision : MonoBehaviour {
    int score;
```

- Modify the method **OnCollisionEnter2D** as follows:

```
if (tag == "pick_me")
{
    Destroy(coll.collider.gameObject);
    score++;
    print ("score" + score);
}
```

In the previous code we increase the score by one every time we collide with a coin; we also print the value of the **score** in the **Console** window.

- Once this is done, please save your script, and check that it is error-free.

- You can also duplicate the object **coin** three times, so that the player can collect more than one object.

- Please run the game and look at the **Console** window to make sure that the score is increased by one every time you collect a coin.

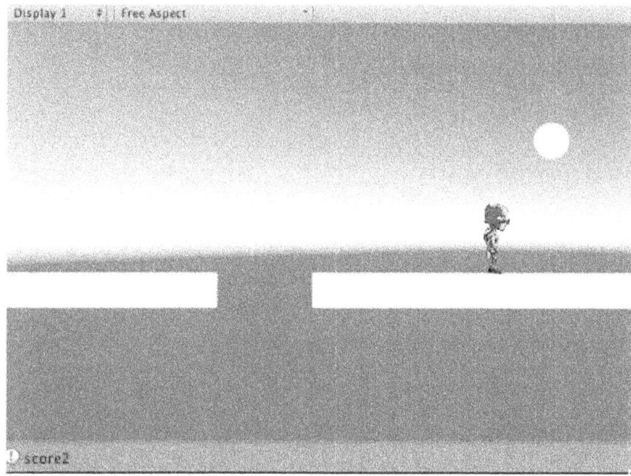

Figure 25: Collecting coins

USING PREFABS

At the moment, we have the basic skeleton for a game with platforms, objects to collect and also objects to avoid; in fact, we could just duplicate one of these two objects several times to complete our level; however, let's say that we want to have 100 coins in the level, and that at some stage we want to modify their attributes (e.g., color, or size); in this case, we would need to modify all these 100 objects, which would be time-consuming; one solution for this, is to create prefabs; prefabs are comparable to templates; you can create a prefab (i.e., a template), create objects based on this template, and modify all these objects at once by only modifying the template; in other words, any change applied to the template will also be applied to the objects based on this template. So let's see how this can be done.

- Please remove the duplicate coins that you have in your scene to keep only one object called **coin**.

- Select this object (i.e., **coin**).

- Drag and drop it to the **Project** window.

- This will create an asset called **coin**, but this time it is **symbolized** by a blue box; this is the usual symbol for a prefab in Unity. If you click on this prefab, you will see, in the **Inspector** window, that it has the exact same properties as the object called **coin** that is present in the **Hierarchy**.

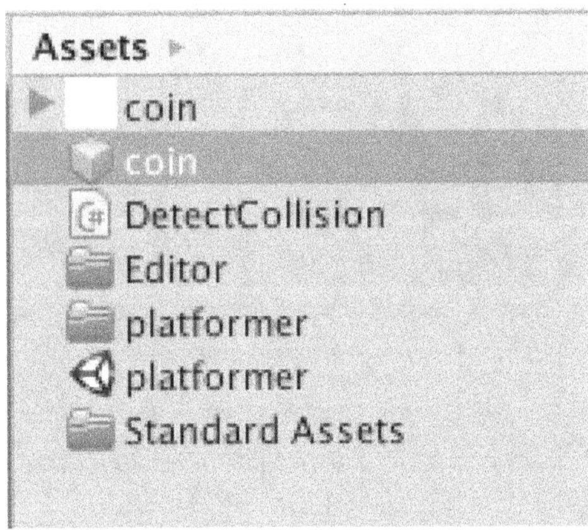

Figure 26: Creating a prefab for the coins

- We can now delete the object called **coin** in the **Hierarchy**.

- Please drag and drop the **coin** prefab from the **Project** window to the **Hierarchy** three times.

- This will create three coins.

Figure 27: Creating objects from a prefab

- Once this is done, please move these coins a few pixels apart in the **Scene** view, as described in the next figure.

Figure 28: Spacing out the new coins

We will now see how to modify their properties at once:

- Please click on the **coin** prefab in the **Project** window.
- Change its color to blue, as described in the next figure.

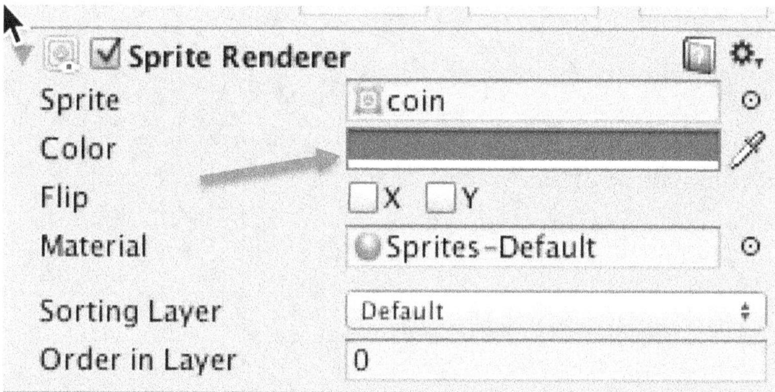

Figure 29: Changing the color of the coin prefab

- You should see that all three coins are now blue. This is because all three are based on the same prefab that we just modified.

Figure 30: Applying the changes to the coin objects

You can also change the prefab's properties from one of the individual coins, for example:

- Select the first coin (object called coin) in the **Hierarchy**.
- Change its color to green using the **Inspector** window.

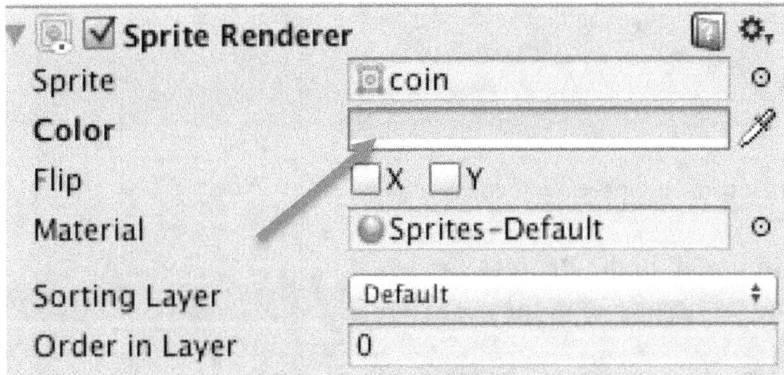

Figure 31: Changing the color of one of the coins

- At this stage only this coin will be green.

Figure 32: Changes applied to one the coins

- However, to apply this green color to all the other coins, you can select the option called **Apply** (top-right corner of the **Inspector**), as described in the next figure.

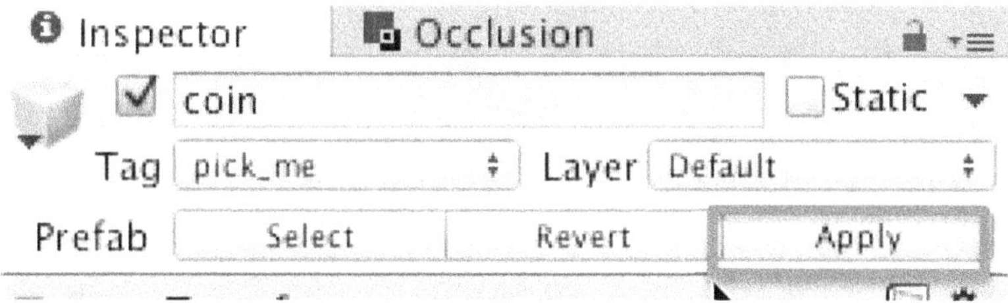

Figure 33: Applying changes to the prefab

- This will **apply** the properties of this particular object to all the other objects based on the same template (i.e., **prefab**).

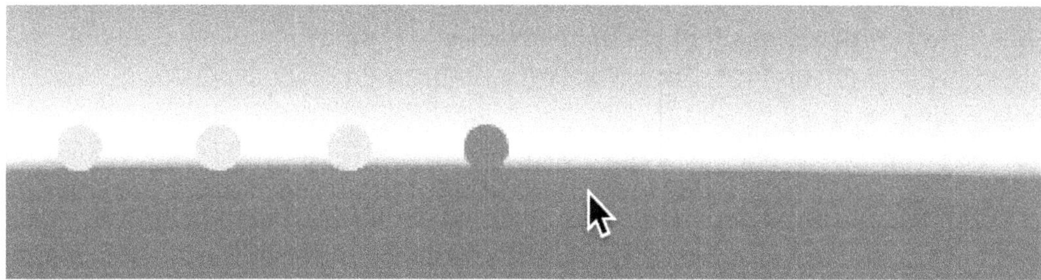

Figure 34: Generalizing the properties to other objects

So, prefabs are very important because they will save you a lot of time, and whenever you create a new feature (or object) that will probably be duplicated in your game, it is good practice to make it a prefab early in the development process.

So, let's apply this principle to the boulder:

- Please drag and drop the **boulder** object to the **Project** window to create a prefab named **boulder**.

- Delete the **boulder** object from the **Hierarchy**.

- Drag and drop the **boulder** prefab to the **Scene** to create a **boulder** object based on this prefab.

- Please duplicate this object **three times**, to roughly have the layout illustrated in the next figure.

Figure 35: Including additional boulders

- Also add two new coins (either duplicates of an existing coin or by dragging and dropping the coin prefab to the scene twice) to the right of the boulders.

Figure 36: Including additional coins

- Please test the scene and check that all the boulders and the coins behave as expected (i.e., the is score increased by one after collecting a coin, or the level is restarted after colliding with a boulder or falling).

Last but not least, we will also create a prefab from our main character so that it can be reused in the next levels (yes, we will be creating several levels :-)).

- Please select the object **CharacterRobotBoy** in the **Hierarchy** window and drag and drop it to the **Project** window; this will create a prefab called **CharacterRobotBoy**.

Figure 37: Creating a prefab from the character

- Once this is done, rename this prefab **player** (i.e., select the prefab, left-click on the name of the prefab, and then modify its name or right-click on the prefab and select **Rename** from the contextual menu); this will also rename the object automatically from **CharacterRobotBoy** to **player** in the **Hierarchy** (since this object is now based on the prefab called **player**).

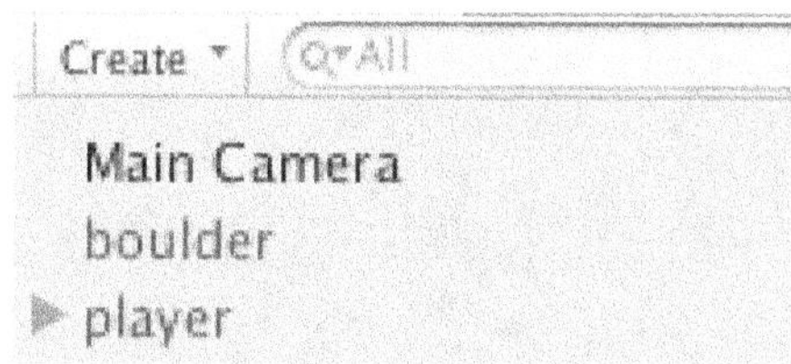

Figure 38: The character and its new name (player)

CREATING A NEW SCENE

Ok, so at this stage we have a level with objects to collect, and a score; what we will do next is to get the player to change level after collecting **five** coins or when the score is **5**.

- First let's save our current scene: select the folder **Assets** in the **Project** window, and then select **File | Save Scene as** from the top menu, and rename the scene **level1**.

The new scene is saved in the active folder; so by selecting a particular folder in the **Project** window before saving a scene, this scene will be saved in this particular folder.

Then, we can create a new scene by duplicating the current scene.

- Please navigate to the folder **Assets** in the **Project** window.

- Select the scene that we have just saved (**level1**).

- Press **CTRL +D** or (**APPLE + D**); this will duplicate the current scene, and the duplicate will be automatically named **level2**.

- You can now open the second level by double-clicking on the scene called **level2** from the **Project** window.

- Unity may ask you if you want to save the current scene (since there were changes since the last time we saved the scene).

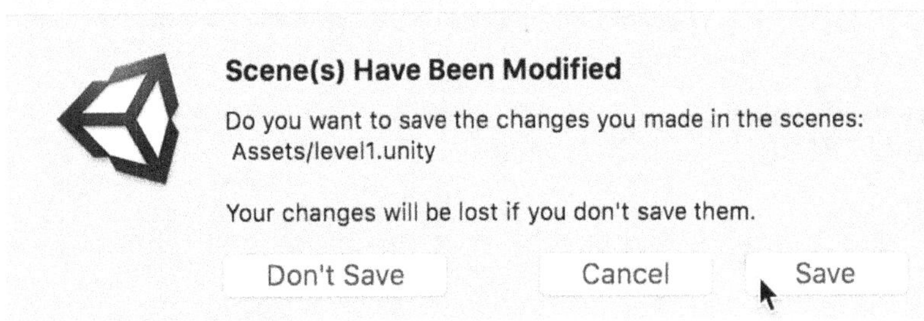

Figure 39: Saving changes made to the scene

- You can click on **Save**, to save your changes.

- You can now check that the current scene is **level2** by looking at the top of the window: the name **level2** should now appear.

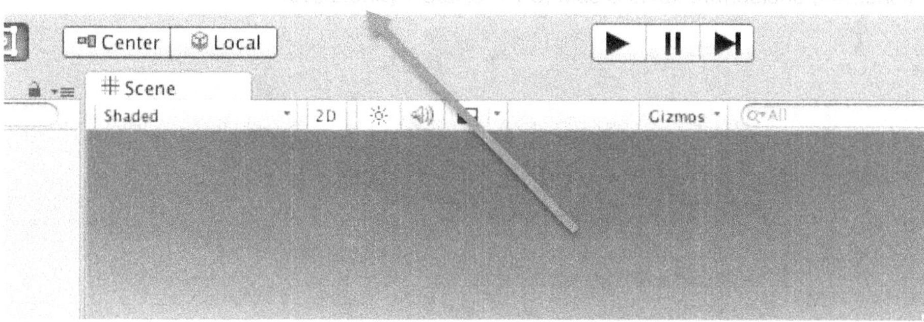

Figure 40: Checking the name of the current scene

Once this is done, we can just remove all coins and boulders from this scene, to only leave the player, the mini-map, and the platforms, for the time being.

- To select all the coins and boulders, you can drag and drop your mouse to select a rectangular area that encompasses all these objects; this will save you some time.

- You can then see that they are all selected either in the **Hierarchy** view, or in the **Scene** view.

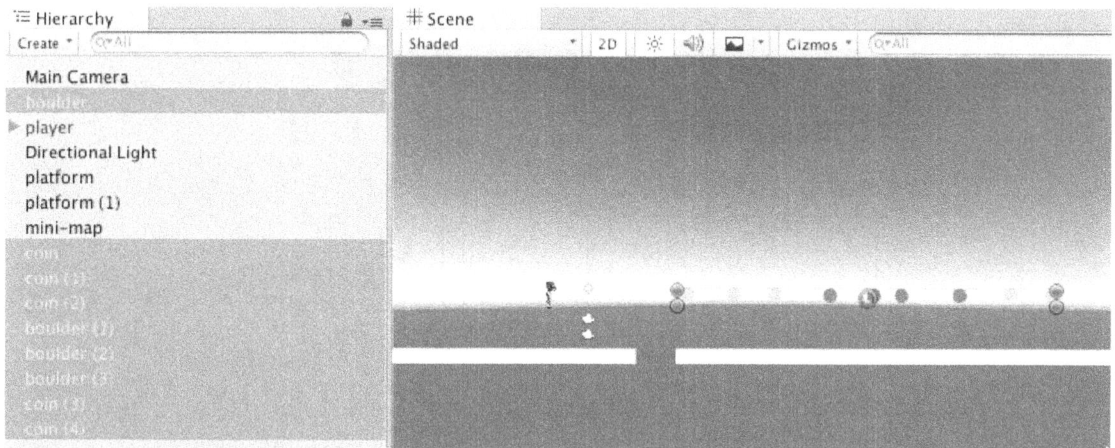

Figure 41: Selecting multiple objects

- Once this is done, you can select and delete these (e.g., **Edit | Delete)**.

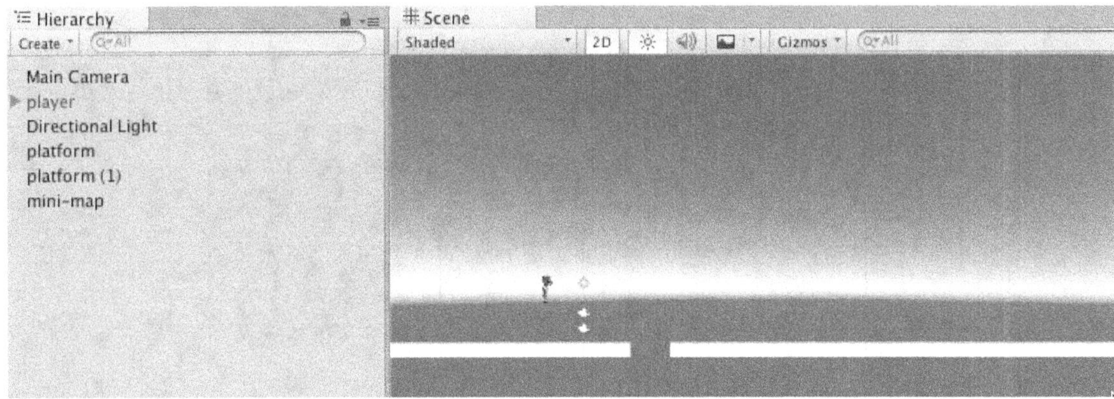

Figure 42: The scene without the coins or boulders

CHANGING LEVEL

Next, we will need to design a mechanism by which we can change level (from **level1** to **level2**) when we have collected **five** coins; this will be done using scripting.

- Please save the current scene (**CTRL + S**) and then open the scene **level1** (i.e., double click on it in the **Project** view).

- Open the script **DetectCollision**.

- Modify the first line of the class as follows:

```
int score, nbCoinsCollectedPerLevel;
```

- Add the following line to the **Start** function:

```
nbCoinsCollectedPerLevel = 0;
```

- Modify the function **OnCollisonEnter2D** as follows (new code in bold):

```
if (tag == "pick_me")
{
     Destroy(coll.collider.gameObject);
     score++;
     nbCoinsCollectedPerLevel++;
     if  (SceneManager.GetActiveScene  ().name  ==  "level1"  &&
nbCoinsCollectedPerLevel >= 5)
     {
          SceneManager.LoadScene ("level2");
     }
     print ("score" + score);


}
```

- In the previous code, we increase the number of coins collected by one, and test whether we have collected five coins; in this case, if the current level is **level1**, we load the scene **level2**.

- Please save the code, and check that it is error-free.

Next, while the code is correct, there is a last thing we need to do; that is: we need to declare the scenes that will be used in our game, so that Unity can load them when we need them; so this will be done using what is called the **Build Settings**.

- Please select **File | Build Settings** from the top menu.

- This will open a new window with this same name.

- You can then drag and drop the scenes **level1** and **level2** from the **Project** window to the **Build Settings** window, as illustrated in the next figure.

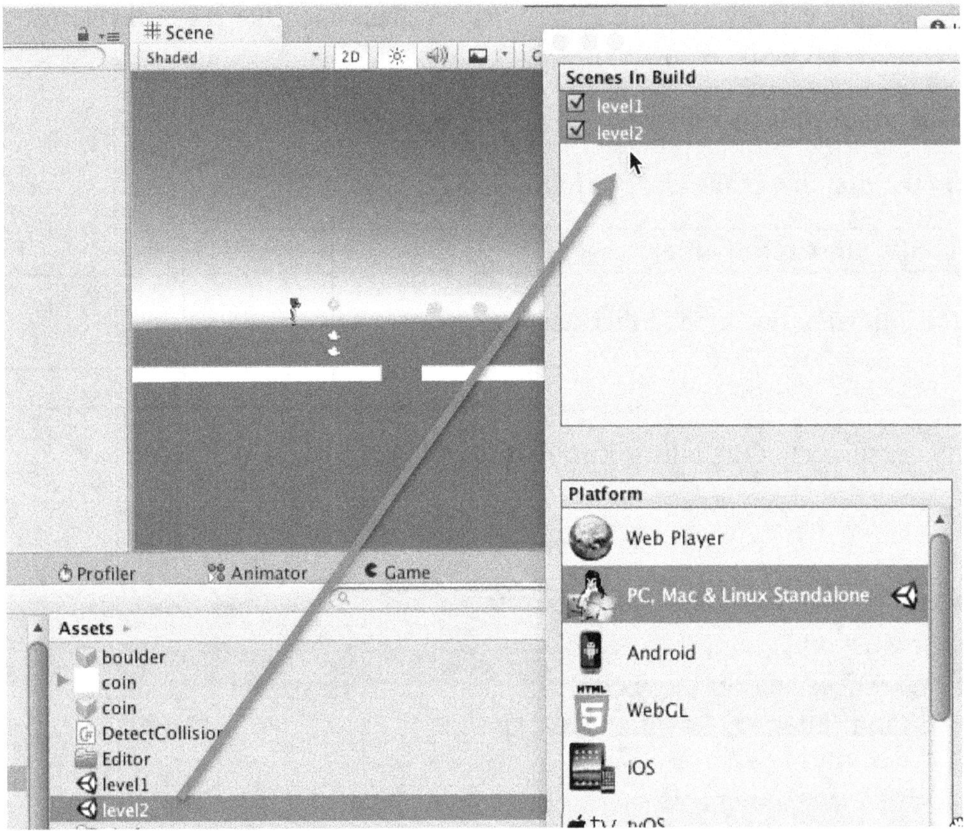

Figure 43: Modifying the build settings

Once this is done, you can close the **Build Settings** window, and test the scene; as you manage to collect five coins, you should transition to the next level (i.e., **level2**).

MANAGING THE NUMBER OF LIVES

At present, we have a score and we can also count the number of coins collected; it would also be nice to be able to use the number of lives, so that the player starts with, for example, three lives, and loses a life whenever s/he falls or hits a boulder.

First, we will create code to check when the player falls; we will then create a mechanism through which the lives are initialized to three, and then decreased after a wrong move was made.

- Please create a new sprite; from the **Project** view, select: **Create | Sprites | Square**.

- Rename this sprite **reStarter**, and drag and drop it to the **Scene** view; this will create a new object called **reStarter**.

- Select this new object (**resSarter**) and, using the **Inspector**, change its position to **(0, -50, 0)** and its scale to **(1000, 1, 1)**. You might need to lower the y-coordinate depending on the starting position of your character.

- You can also deactivate its **SpriteRenderer** component, as illustrated on the next figure.

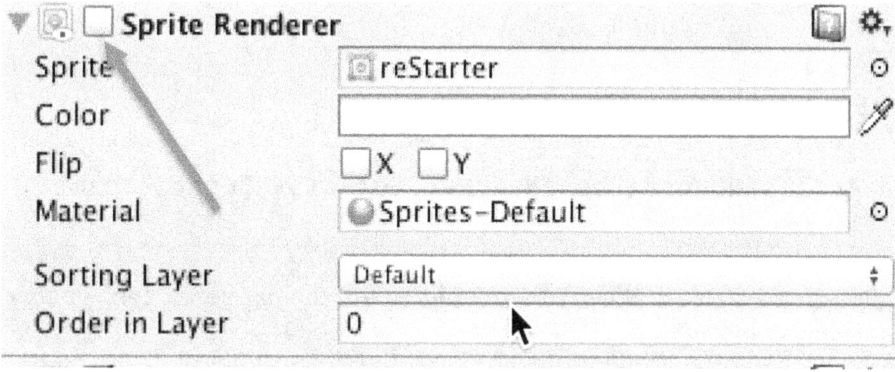

Figure 44: Deactivating the Sprite Renderer

- Please create a new tag (as we have done earlier) called **reStarter** and apply it to this object.

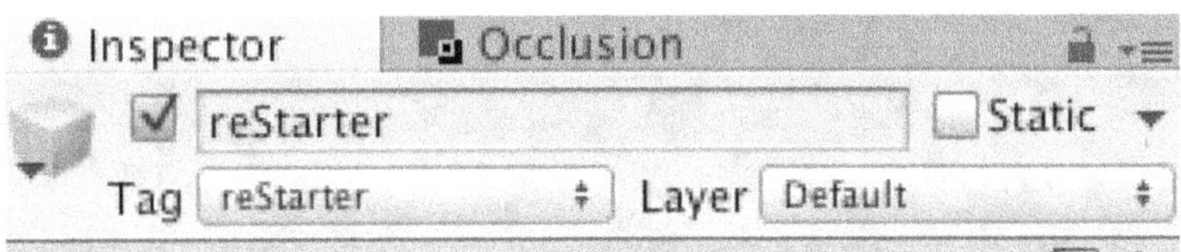

Figure 45: Adding a new tag reStarter

- The last thing will be to add a collider to this object: please select **Component | Physics2D | BoxCollider2D**.

So this object, although it won't be visible, will be collidable, and will be used to detect when the player is low enough that we can assume that it is falling.

The last thing we need to do is to modify our collision detection script to detect when the player collides with this object **reStarter**; in this case, we will restart the current level, as we have done for the collision with the boulders.

- Please open the script **DetectCollision**.

- Add the following code to it (new code in bold).

```
if (tag == "avoid_me")
{
     Destroy(coll.collider.gameObject);
     SceneManager.LoadScene(SceneManager.GetActiveScene().name);
}
if (tag == "reStarter")
{
     SceneManager.LoadScene(SceneManager.GetActiveScene().name);
}
```

- In the previous code, if we collide with an object with the tag **reStarter**, we then reload the current scene.

- Once this is done, check your code, and play the scene. Get the character to jump from a platform, and see as it is falling, that the level restarts automatically.

Once you have checked that this feature is working, you can create a prefab from the object **reStarter** by dragging and dropping this object to the **Project** window.

COMPLETING THE STRUCTURE OF OUR GAME

In the next sections, we will get to complete the skeleton of our game, by including, a **splash-screen**, **level1**, **level2** and a **game-over** or **win** screen. If the player manages to collect five coins, s/he will evolve to **level2**; then in **level2**, if s/he reaches the end of the level by jumping on platforms, s/he will win. The player will lose if s/he runs out of lives.

So let's complete the second scene, it will be a simple scene with platforms, a few pixels apart, that the player has to reach to complete the level.

- Please open the scene **level2**.

- Drag and drop the prefab **reStarter** from the **Project** window to the **Scene** view, this will create a new object called **reStarter**.

- Change its position to **(0, -50, 0)**.

We will now create a succession of small platforms that the player will need to jump on.

- Please select the platform to the right of the player (i.e., **platform1**).

- Change its scale to **(3.5, 1, 1)**.

- Rename it **small_platform**, and create a prefab with it, by dragging and dropping this object to the **Project** window.

Once this is done, you can duplicate this object (i.e., the small platform) seven times to create seven additional platforms that you can place side by side with some space in between, as illustrated on the next figure.

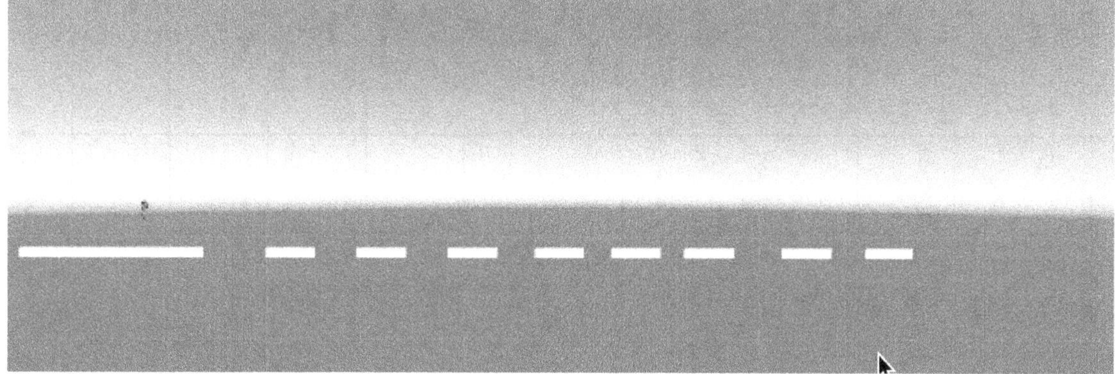

Figure 46: Adding small platforms

We can then do the following:

- Select the platform just below the player (i.e., the long platform) and rename it **long_platform**.

- Create a prefab from it (as we have done previously).

- Duplicate the object **long_platform** and move the duplicate to the right of the last small platform to obtain the layout that is illustrated in the next figure.

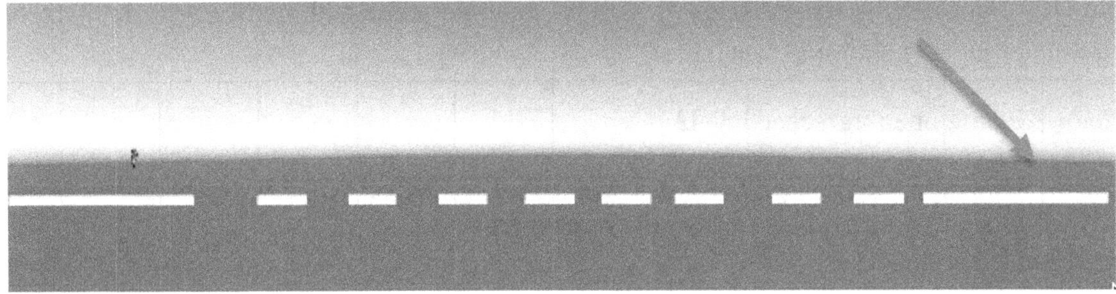

Figure 47: Completing the second level

To add some rewards, we can also include a few coins to the scene, above every small platform, by dragging and dropping the prefab called **coin** from the **Project** window to the **Scene** view several times.

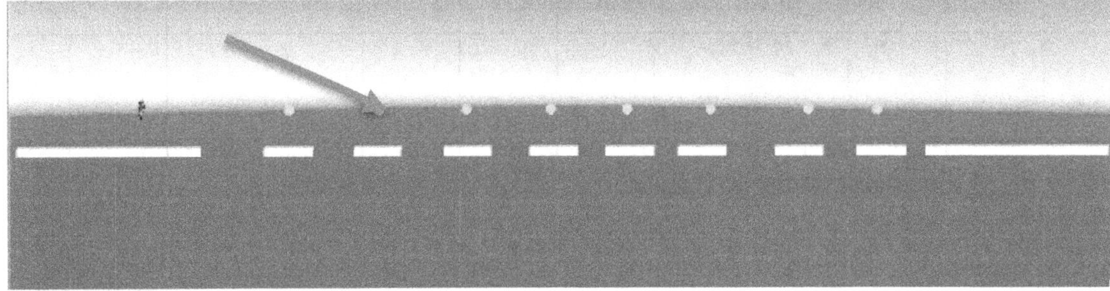

Figure 48: Adding coins

The last thing is to is to create an object that symbolizes the end of **level2**; it will be used to transfer the user to the **win** screen (that we yet have to create).

Please do the following:

- Create a new triangle sprite: from the **Project** view, select **Create | Sprites | Triangle**.

- This will create a new sprite in the **Project** view.

- Rename it **endOfLevel2**.

- Once this is done, you can drag and drop it to the **Scene** view so that it appears to the right of the second long platform (as illustrated on the next figure).

- This will create a new object called **endOfLevelTwo**.

- You can then change the color of this object to green, using the **Inspector** window, by modifying its component called **Sprite Renderer**.

- We can also change its rotation to **(0, 0, -90)** and its scale to **(3, 3, 1)**.

Figure 49: Creating the end of the level

- Finally, we will add a collider to this object by selecting **Component | Physics2D | BoxCollider2D**.
- You can now test your scene. As you reach the end of the level, you will collide with the object **endOfLevel2** (i.e., the green triangle); however, nothing will happen (i.e., no transition to the win screen) since we have not coded this feature yet.

To finish the basic structure of our game, we will be adding a splash-screen and an end screen.

CREATING A SPLASH SCREEN

Our splash screen will be the first screen displayed for our game; it will consist of a background image and a button.

- Please save the current scene (**File | Save Scene**).

- Create a new Scene (**File | New Scene**) and rename it **splashScreen** (**File | Save Scene As…**).

- By default, this new scene will include a camera and a light.

First we will create a button that will be used to load the first scene.

So let's create this button:

- Please select: **GameObject | UI | Button**. This will create a new button along with an object called **Canvas**.

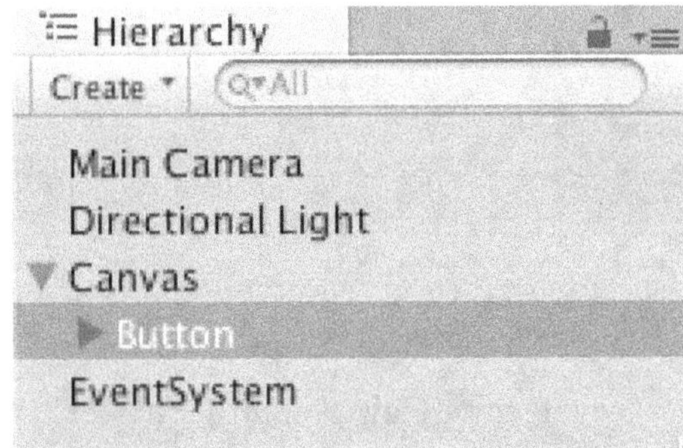

Figure 50: Creating a new button

- You can focus the view on this button by double-clicking on the button in the **Hierarchy** (or by selecting the button and then pressing *SHIFT + F*).

- This should display the button, along with a white rectangle that marks the boundary of the screen view.

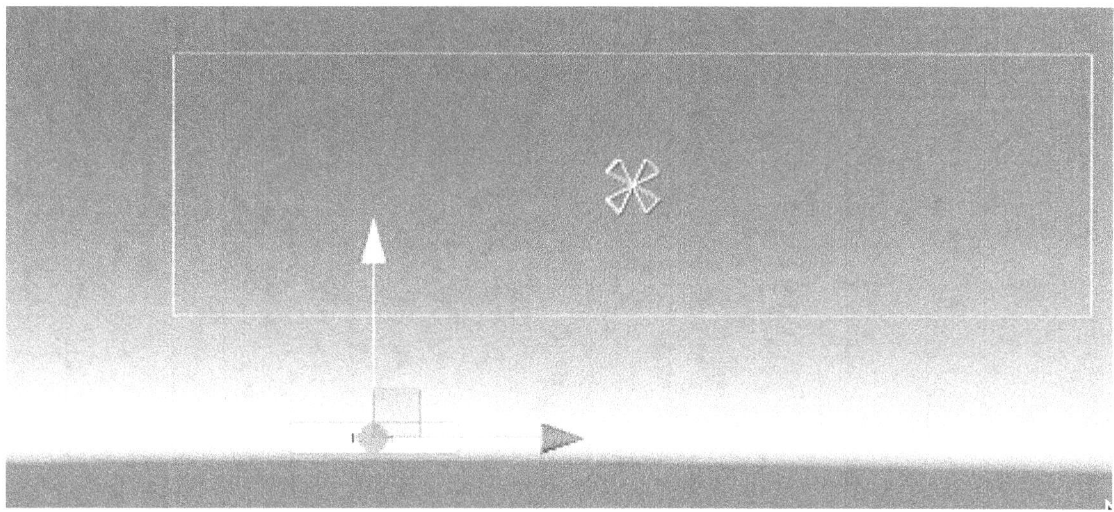

Figure 51: Focusing on the button

- Please move the button to the center of the white rectangle or, using the **Inspector**, change the **PosX**, **PosY** and **PosZ** properties of its **Rect Transform** component to **(0, 0, 0)**, as illustrated on the next figure.

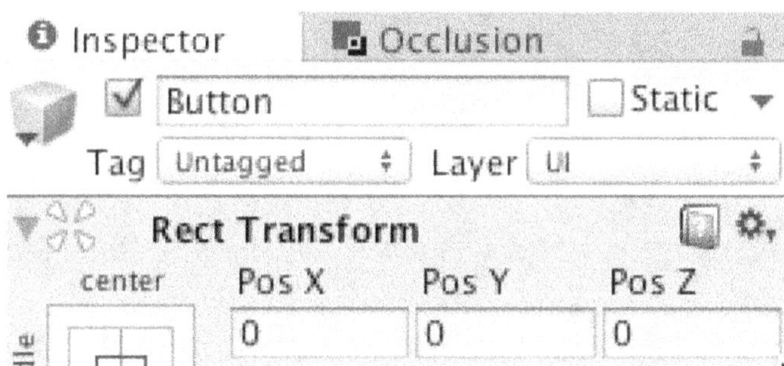

Figure 52: Changing the position of the button (part 1)

- The button should now be in the middle of the screen.

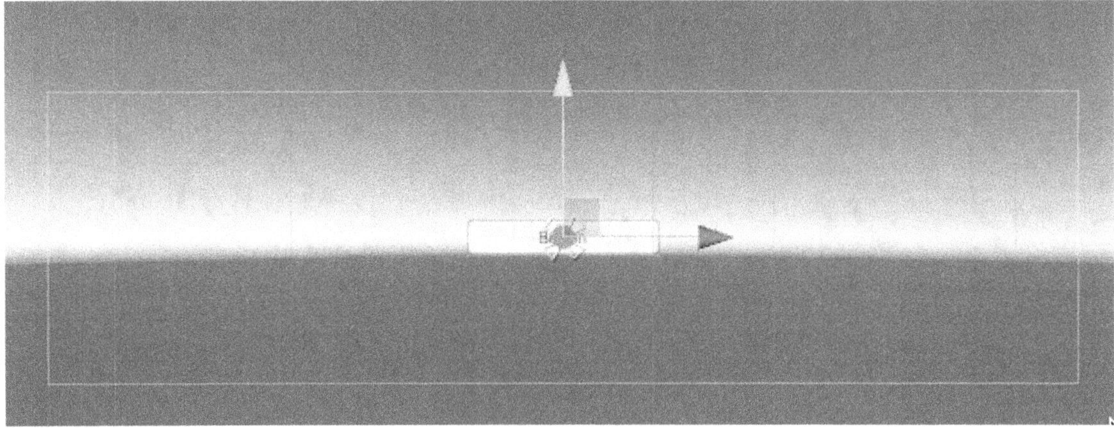

Figure 53: Changing the position of the button (part 2)

We can now change the text displayed on the button:

- Using the **Hierarchy**, select the object called **Text** that is a child of the object called **Button**.

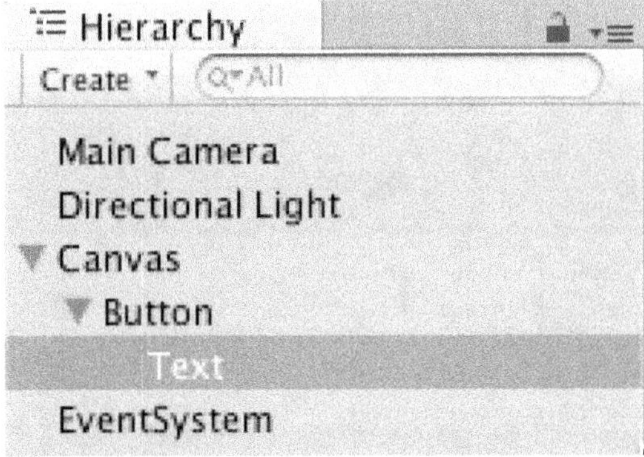

Figure 54: Selecting the text of the button

- Using the **Inspector**, you can change the **Text** property of the component called **Text** to **"Start"**.

Figure 55: Changing the label of the button

Once this is done, we will start to create a script that will be used to change levels.

- Please create a new C# script and name it **ControlButtons**.

- Open this script.

- Add this code at the start of the file.

```
using UnityEngine.SceneManagement;
```

- Add the following code within the class.

```
public void startLevel1()
{
    SceneManager.LoadScene("level1");
}
```

In the previous code, we create a new function called **startLevel1**; when this function is called, it will load the scene called **level1**.

Once this is done:

- Please save your code.

- Check that it is error-free.

- Create a new empty object (**GameObject | Create Empty**) and rename it **manageButtons**.

- Drag and drop the script **ControlButtons** to this empty object (i.e., the object **manageButtons**).

Last, we will select an action to be performed whenever the user clicks on the button.

- Click once on the button (called **Button**) in the **Hierarchy.**

- In the **Inspector** window, scroll down to the section called **Button** (i.e., at the bottom of the **Inspector** window).

- Click on the + sign below the text **"List is Empty"**.

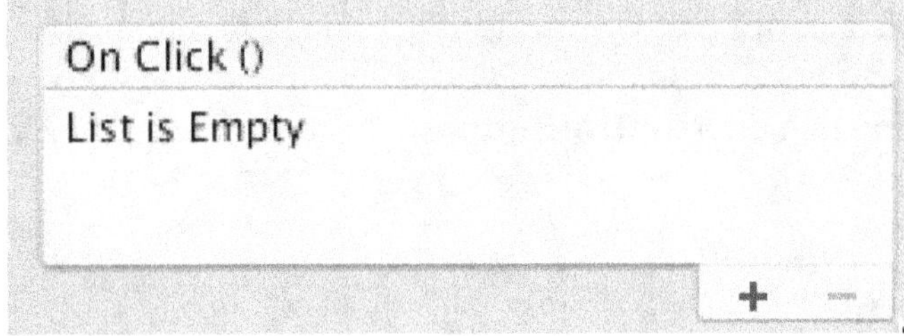

Figure 56: Adding a new event handler

- This will reveal new attributes.

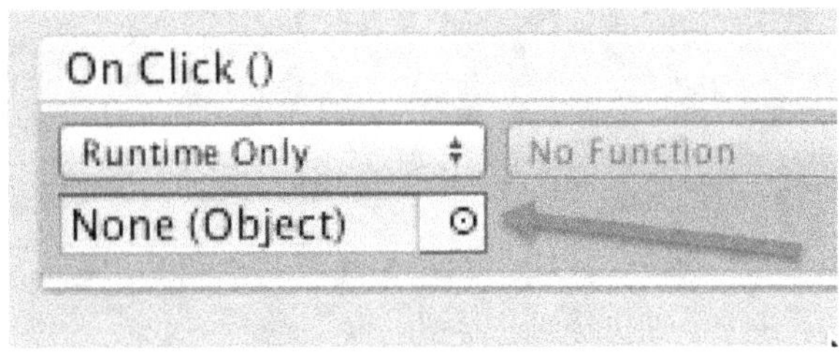

Figure 57: Displaying new attributes for the button

- You can now drag and drop the object called **manageButtons**, from the **Hierarchy** view, to the field labelled as **"None (Object)"**.

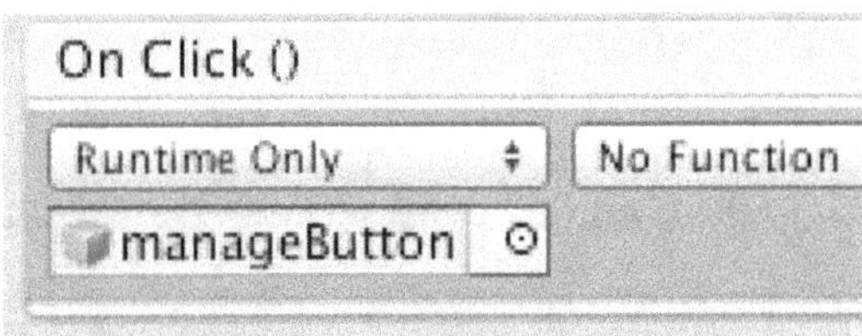

Figure 58: Adding the empty object to the button

For this to work, you need to drag the empty object to the field **None (Object)**, but NOT the script. In other words, if you drag and drop the script to this field, you will not be able to access it functions; instead, you need to drag and drop an empty object that includes the script **ControlButtons**. This will then give access to the functions within the script.

- Once this is done, click on the label **"No function"** and select **ControlButtons | StartLevel1** from the drop down menu.

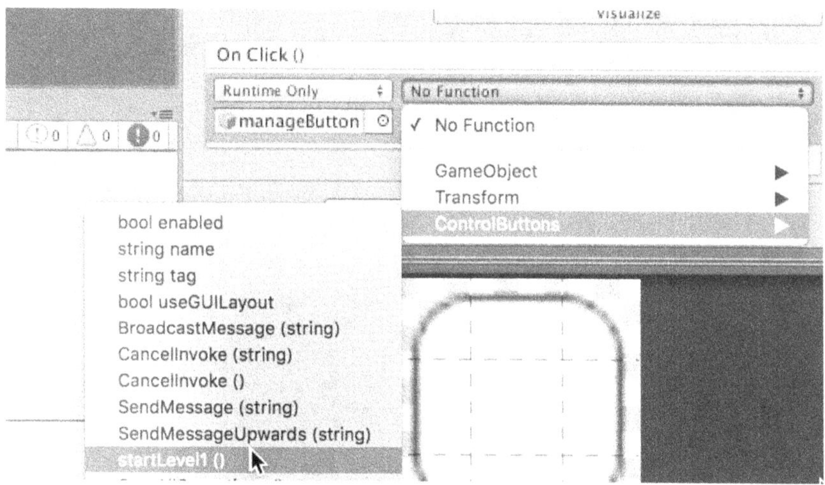

Figure 59: Selecting the function to be called (part 1)

- By doing this, we effectively tell the system that in case the user clicks on the button, the function **startLevel1**, that is included in the script (or class) **ControlButtons**, should be called.

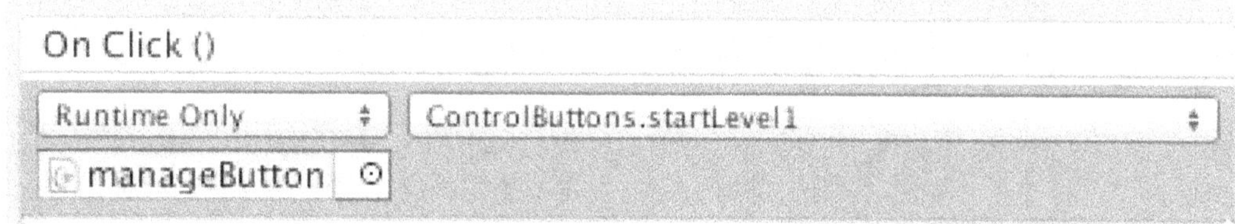

Figure 60: Selecting the function to be called (part 2)

Last, but not least, we just need to include this scene to the **Build Settings**, by opening the corresponding window (**File | Build Settings**) and clicking on the button **Add Open Scenes**.

Figure 61: Adding the current scene to the Build Settings

In the previous figure, you can see that all the scenes listed have an associated number (to the right) that indicates the order in which they will appear in the game; so we could also drag and drop the splash-screen scene in this view from the third to the first position in this list, as described in the next figure.

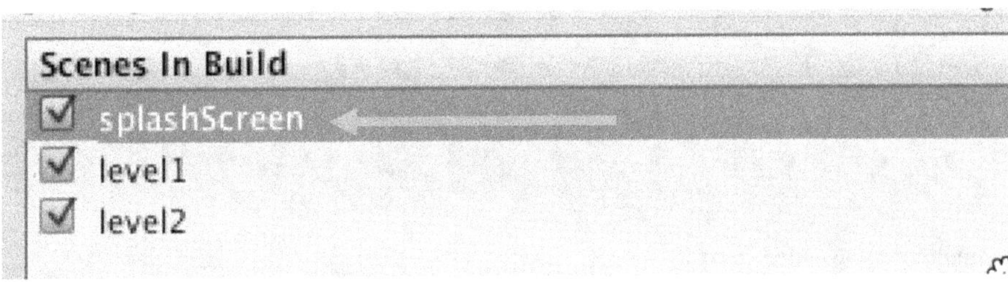

Figure 62: Moving the splash-screen to the first position

- We can now close the **Build Settings** window, and test our button. As you play the scene and click on the button, the first level (**level1**) should be loaded.

CREATING THE END SCREENS (WIN AND LOSE)

We will now create the last two screens for the skeleton of our game: a screen when the player wins (after reaching the end of the second level) and a screen for when the player loses after s/he has no more lives. Note that we have not dealt with the management of lives yet, and this will be done just after this section.

- Please save the current scene (**Files | Save Scene**).

- Create a new Scene (**File | New Scene**).

- Save this scene as **win** (**File | Save Scene As**).

- Add a new **UI Text** object (**GameObject | UI | Text**). This will create a new object called **Text**, as illustrated on the next figure.

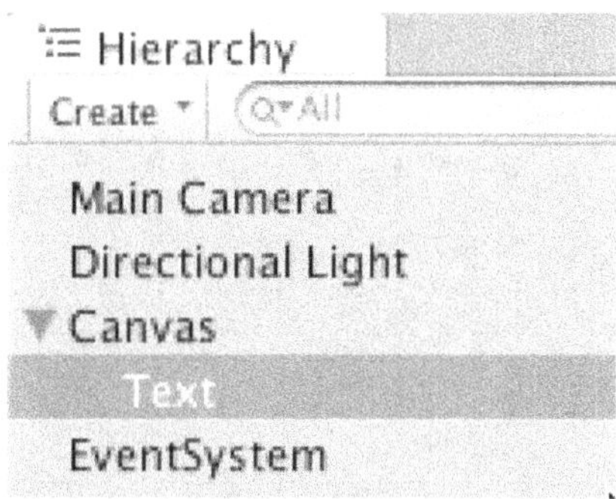

Figure 63: Adding a text UI object

Select this new object called **Text**, and, using the **Inspector**, change its attributes as follows:

- Component **RectTransform**: **width = 500**; **height = 200**; **Anchor Preset** (the box just below the label **Rect Transform**) = **Middle - center**.

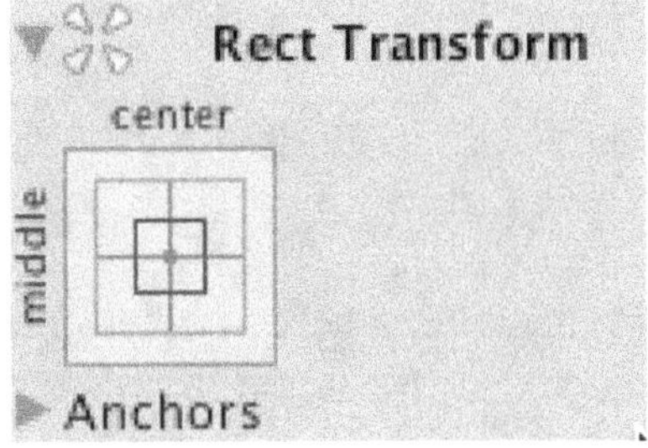

Figure 64: Modifying the RectTransform component

- Component **Text Script**: Text = "Well Done!"; Font-Style = Bold; Font-Size = 91; Color=Green; paragraph alignment (middle-center).

Figure 65: Modifying the Paragraph component

Figure 66: Displaying the text after the changes

Once this is done, we will just create a button that will be used to restart the game.

- Please create a button as we have done previously (**GameObject | UI | Button**).

- Using the **Move** tool, move this button below the text that you have just created.

- Select the **Text** object that is a child of this button in the **Hierarchy**.

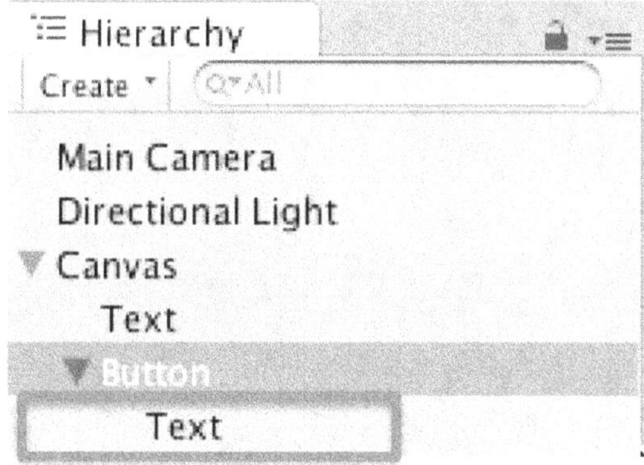

Figure 67: Selecting the label for the button

- Using the **Inspector**, change the text attribute of the **Text** component for this object to >> **Restart Game**<<.

Once this is done, we just need to modify our previous class **ControlButtons**, to include a function that loads the splash-screen, and we can then attach this script to an empty object.

- Please open the script **ControlButtons**.

- Add the following code to the class (at the end).

```
public void loadSplashScreen()
{
    SceneManager.LoadScene("splashScreen");
}
```

- In the previous code, we declare the function **loadSplashScreen** that will load the scene called **splashScreen** when it is called.

- Please save your code.

- Create an empty object called **manageButtons**.

- Drag and drop the script called **ControlButtons** to this empty object.

- Add this scene (i.e., **win**) to the **Build Settings**.

Figure 68: Adding the scene to the Build Settings

Next, we will define the function that is called when this button is pressed.

- Click once on the button in the **Hierarchy.**

- In the **Inspector** window, scroll down to the section called **Button** (i.e., bottom of the **Inspector** window).

- Click on the + sign below the text **"List is Empty"**.

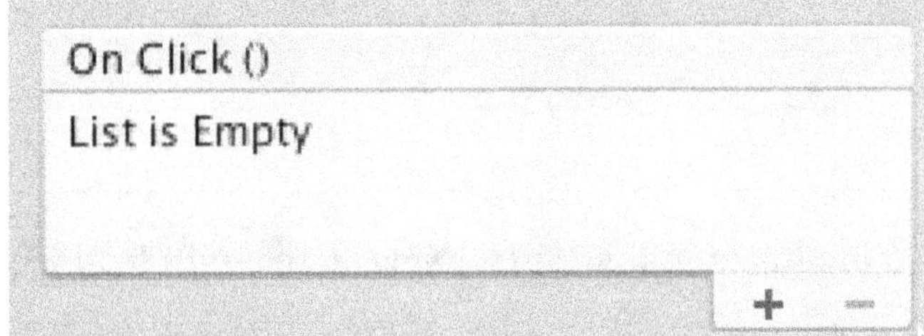

Figure 69: Selecting an event handler (part 1)

- This will reveal new attributes.

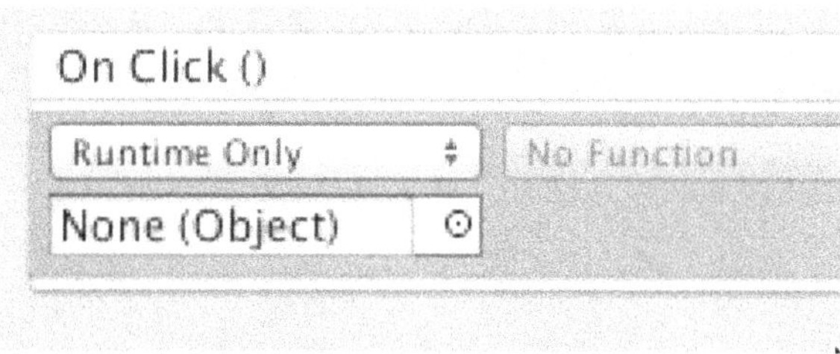

Figure 70: Selecting an event handler (part 2)

- You can now drag and drop the object called **manageButtons**, from the **Hierachy** view, to the field labelled as "**None (Object)**".

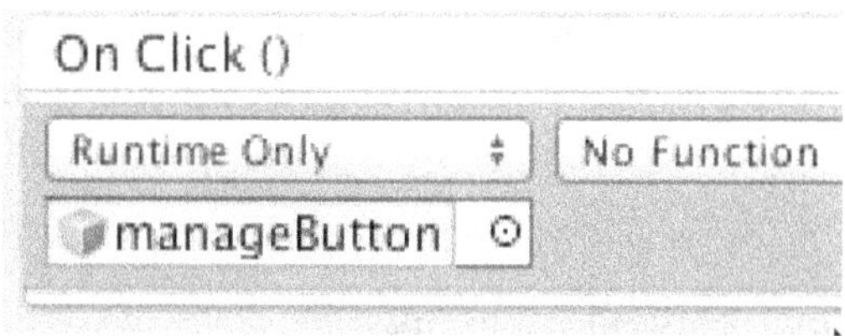

Figure 71: Selecting a function (part 1)

- Once this is done, click on the label "**No function**" and select **ControlButtons | LoadSplashScreen**.

By doing this, we effectively tell the system that in case the user clicks on the button, the function **loadSplahScreen**, that is included in the script (or class) **ControlButtons**, should be called.

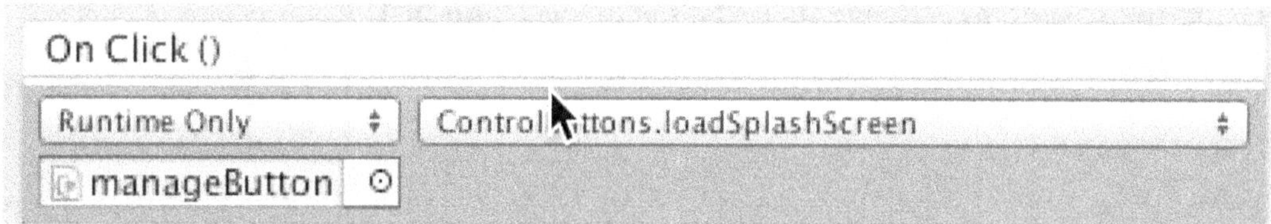

Figure 72: Selecting a function (part 2)

- You can now test the scene and check that by clicking on the button, you are redirected to the splash-screen.

We can now create a prefab from the object **manageButtons**, as the scripts within will be used later on:

- Please drag and drop the object **manageButtons** to the **Project** view, this will create a prefab called **manageButtons**.

Figure 73: The new prefab manageButtons

Once this is done, we just need to create a new scene for when the player loses; this will be quite identical to the **win** scene, except from the message displayed onscreen.

- Please save the current scene (**File | Save Scene**).

- Duplicate this scene (i.e., the **win** scene): from the **Project** view, select the scene called **win** and duplicate it *(CTRL + D or APPLE + D)*; rename the duplicate **lose** (i.e., click once on it then change its name, or select it and press **Enter**), this will be the scene used when the player loses.

- In the **Project** view, double-click on the scene called **lose** to open it.

- Once the scene is open, using the **Hierarchy**, select the object called **Text**, that is a child of the object **canvas**.

Figure 74: Selecting the Text object

- Using the **Inspector**, change its text attribute to "**You lost!**"

- The button's label does not need to be changed since it will also ask the player to restart the game.

The only thing that we need to do now is to add this scene to the **Build Settings** by opening the **Build Settings** window (**File| Build Settings**), and by then selecting the option **Add Open Scenes**.

Figure 75: Adding a new scene to the Build Settings

That's it. We can now close the **Build Settings** window, and the last thing we can do is to make sure that the **win** scene is displayed when the player reaches the end of the second level.

So let's proceed:

- Please open the scene called **level2**.

- Select the object **endOfLevelTwo**.

- Create a new tag (as we have done previously) called **endOfLevelTwo** and apply it to this object.

- Open the script **DetectCollision**.

- Add this code at the end of the function **OnCollisionEnter2D**.

```
if (tag == "endOfLevelTwo")
{
    SceneManager.LoadScene("win");
}
```

- Please save your code.

- Play the scene (**level2**) and make sure that the **win** screen is displayed once the player reaches the end of the level.

LEVEL ROUNDUP

Well, this is it!

In this chapter, we have learned about creating a simple splash-screen, adding buttons, processing clicks on buttons, and changing levels; in the process, we also learned how to use prefabs to optimize your time. We have, by now, a very simple, but almost complete, platform game with two levels, along with the out-of-game screens (i.e., win, lose, and splash-screen).

Checklist

You can consider moving to the next chapter if you can do the following:

- Duplicate a scene.

- Create a prefab.

- Create an object based on a prefab.

- Create a button and the corresponding code to detect a click on it.

- Know how to access and use the **Build Settings**.

Quiz

It's now time to check your knowledge with a quiz. So please try to answer the following questions (or specify whether the statements are correct or incorrect). The solutions are included in your resource pack. Good luck!

1. You can duplicate a scene by selecting it in the **Project** view and by then pressing *CTRL + D*.

2. If a scene is called **level1**, its duplicate will automatically be renamed **level2** (unless **level2** exists already).

3. A prefab can be created by selecting an object in the **Hierarchy** and by then pressing *CTRL + P*.

4. You can create a new button, by selecting **GameObject | Button** from the top menu.

5. You can create a new button, by selecting **GameObject | Text** from the top menu.

6. In the **Build-Settings** window, the number to the right of each scene indicates the order in which it would usually appear in the game.

7. For a scene to be loaded from a script, this scene has to be included in the **Build Settings**.

8. So that something happens when a button is clicked, a function needs to be selected using the **Inspector**.

9. To modify the label of a button, you can change the text object that is a child of this button.

10. Whenever the first **UI** object of a scene is added to this scene, an object called **canvas** is also created.

Challenge 1

Now that you have managed to complete this chapter and that you have improved your skills, let's do the following.

- Add a **Text UI** object to the splash-screen, above the **Start** button, with the title of the game.

- Create a new scene called **Instructions** (e.g., duplicate the **splash-screen** scene).

- Add a button called <<**Back** to this scene. Upon clicking on this button the player should go back to the splash-screen.

- Add a button called **Instructions** to the splash-screen. Upon clicking on this button the player should go to the scene called **Instructions**.

Challenge 2

In this challenge, you will be adding a new background to the splash-screen

- Import the texture called **RobotBoy** from the resource pack (or use any texture of your choice).

- Create a new canvas: select **GameObject | UI | Canvas**.

- Select this canvas.

- Using the Inspector, change its **Sort Order** attribute (in the component called **Canvas**) to **-1**; this will ensure that any UI object within this canvas is displayed behind the button (the **Sort Order** of the canvas used for the button is 0 by default).

- Create a new **RawImage:** select **GameObject | UI | Raw Image** from the top menu, and make sure that this image is a child of the new canvas that you have created

- Modify the position and scale of this image, so that it fills the screen.

- Test your scene.

3

ADDING SOUND AND DISPLAYING VALUES ONSCREEN

In this section, we will discover how to display the score and the number of lives onscreen, as well as how to be able to access these variables throughout the game.

After completing this chapter, you will be able to:

- Display and update text onscreen.

- Store and access information saved in the player preferences.

- Keep objects across scenes.

- Display or hide text depending on the current scene.

- Create a background music and sound effects.

- Play one or multiple sounds.

[78]

INTRODUCTION

In this chapter we will improve the current game by adding a few tweaks that will make it more enjoyable and easy-to-play. We will start by keeping the score (and the number of lives) between scenes, so that the game does not reset these values at the start of every level; instead of displaying the score and the number of lives in the **Console** window, we will get to display them onscreen thanks to **UI Text** objects, so that the user can see this information at a glance. Finally, we will add some background music to our scenes

MANAGING LIVES AND SCORE THROUGHOUT THE GAME

Ok, so at this point we have several levels, and the skeleton of our platform game, including a **splash-screen**, a **win** screen and a **lose** screen; we also keep track of the score and the number of lives.

Now, about these two: although we have created variables to keep track of the number of lives and the score, the following issue remains: the score is usually reset at the start of each level because it is declared and initialised in the **Start** function which is called whenever the scene starts; so we need to keep track of these variables throughout the game.

The first way we could do this is to create an **nbLives** variable in the **DetectCollision** script, initialize it to three in the **Start** function, and then decrease its value every time we restart the level; however, there are two issues with this approach: whenever we go to the next scene, this number of lives will be reset to zero; in fact, this would be the same for the score; so we need to find a way to be able to store data that will be kept as we move from one scene to the next.

This can be done with what is called the **Player Preferences**. Using **Player Preferences**, you can store information in variables of types integer, boolean, or string, that will be accessible (and maintained) throughout the game.

So, using the **Player Preferences**, we will do the following:

- Set the score (in the player preferences) to 0 and the number of lives to 3 in the splash-screen.

- The score (in the player preferences) and the number of lives will be updated in every scene, by accessing the player preferences, reading the current number of lives or the score, and modifying this value.

So let's get started:

- Please open the **splashScreen** scene.

- Create an empty object called **initGame**.

- Then create a new C# script called **initGame**: from the **Project** window, please select **Create | C# Script** and rename this script **initGame**.

- Open this script and modify the **Start** function as follows:

```
void Start ()
{
     PlayerPrefs.SetInt("score",0);
     PlayerPrefs.SetInt("nbLives",3);
}
```

In the previous code:

- We create the variable **score** that is stored in the player preferences; it can be considered as a global variable as it is accessible throughout the game; it is set to **0**.

- The same is done with the variable **nbLives** that is set to **3**.

- Once you have saved your script and checked that it is error-free, you can drag and drop it to the object **initGame**.

Next, we need to use these variables throughout the game, especially when the player collects items or loses a life by falling or colliding with dangerous objects.

- Please save your scene, and then open the scene called **level1**.

- Open the script called **DetectCollision**.

- Replace this line…

```
int score, nbCoinsCollectedPerLevel;
```

with this line…

```
int score, nbLives, nbCoinsCollectedPerLevel;
```

- Then, in the **Start** function, you can comment the line that sets the score to 0, as follows:

```
//score = 0;
```

- We can then modify the code that deals with the **score** as follows (new code in bold):

```
if (tag == "pick_me")
{
      Destroy(coll.collider.gameObject);
      //score++;
      score = PlayerPrefs.GetInt("score");
      score++;
      PlayerPrefs.SetInt("score", score)
```

In the previous code:

- We comment the line that used to increase the local score by 1.

- We then fetch the value of the **score** that is stored in the player preferences.

- We increase this value by one, and save the new value in the player preferences.

We now need to modify the code that deals with the number of lives; please add the following code to the script **DetectCollision**:

```
if (tag == "avoid_me" || tag == "reStarter")
{
      Destroy(coll.collider.gameObject);
      nbLives = PlayerPrefs.GetInt("nbLives");
      nbLives--;
      PlayerPrefs.SetInt("nbLives", nbLives);
      if             (nbLives              >=              0)
SceneManager.LoadScene(SceneManager.GetActiveScene().name);
      else SceneManager.LoadScene("lose");
      print ("lives" + nbLives);
}
/*if (tag == "reStarter")
{
      SceneManager.LoadScene(SceneManager.GetActiveScene().name);

}*/
```

In the previous code:

- We have grouped the two conditional statements that checked for collision with a **reStarter** object or a boulder (i.e., tag = **avoid_me**).

- In this case, we decrease the current number of lives by accessing its value from the player preferences, decreasing the value, and updating the player preferences accordingly.

- We also commented the code that used to be employed to detect the tag **reStarter**, since this is now done in the code just above (i.e., in the combined conditional statement).

Once this has been done, please save your code, check that it is error-free, and test the game as follows:

- Save the current scene.

- Open the scene called **splashScreen**.

- Play the game and proceed to the first level.

- Test that if you fall, the number of lives displayed in the **Console** window is correct and that after 3 falls, you are redirected to the scene called **lose**.

- Check that your score is kept when you go from the first scene to the second scene.

REMOVING ERRONEOUS MESSAGES

As it is, you may have noticed that every time you play the scene, there is a message in the **Console** window saying "**There are two audio listeners in the scene...**"; this is because we use two cameras, each using one **Audio Listener**; however, we only need to have one audio listener in each scene; so we just need to deactivate one of these audio listeners as follows:

- Please open the scene called **level1**.

- Please select the camera called **mini-map** in the **Hierarchy**.

- Using the **Inspector** window, deactivate its **Audio Listener** component.

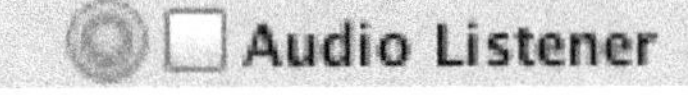

Figure 76: Deactivating the Audio Listener component

- Please do the same in the scene called **level2**.

- If you play the game again, this error message should have disappeared.

ADDING A USER INTERFACE

Ok; so far so good; we can keep our score and number of lives between scenes. The next step will be to display the number of lives and the score onscreen for the player. For this, we will create what are called **UI elements** and update them accordingly when the score or number of lives have been changed; and since these (the UI for the score and the number of lives) will be used across all scenes, we will also learn how to create them once and then keep them for all the out-of-game scenes (i.e., the scenes where there is no game play and that consist of menu and buttons).

So let's get started:

- Please open the scene **level1**.

- Select: **GameObject | UI | Text**; this will create a text object, that we can use for the score, named **Text**.

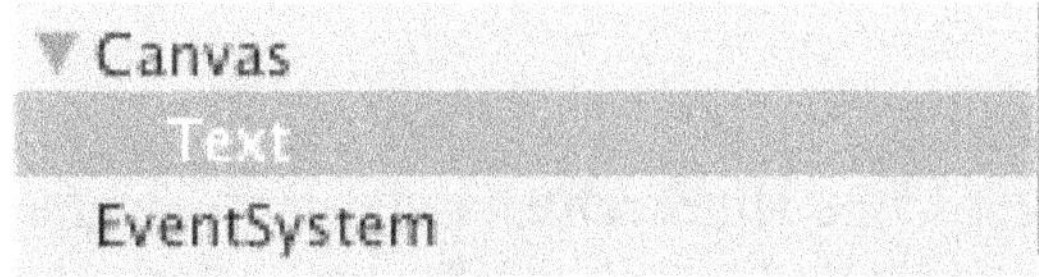

Figure 77: Adding a Text UI

You can rename it **scoreUI** and move it in the top-left corner of the white rectangle that defines the game window.

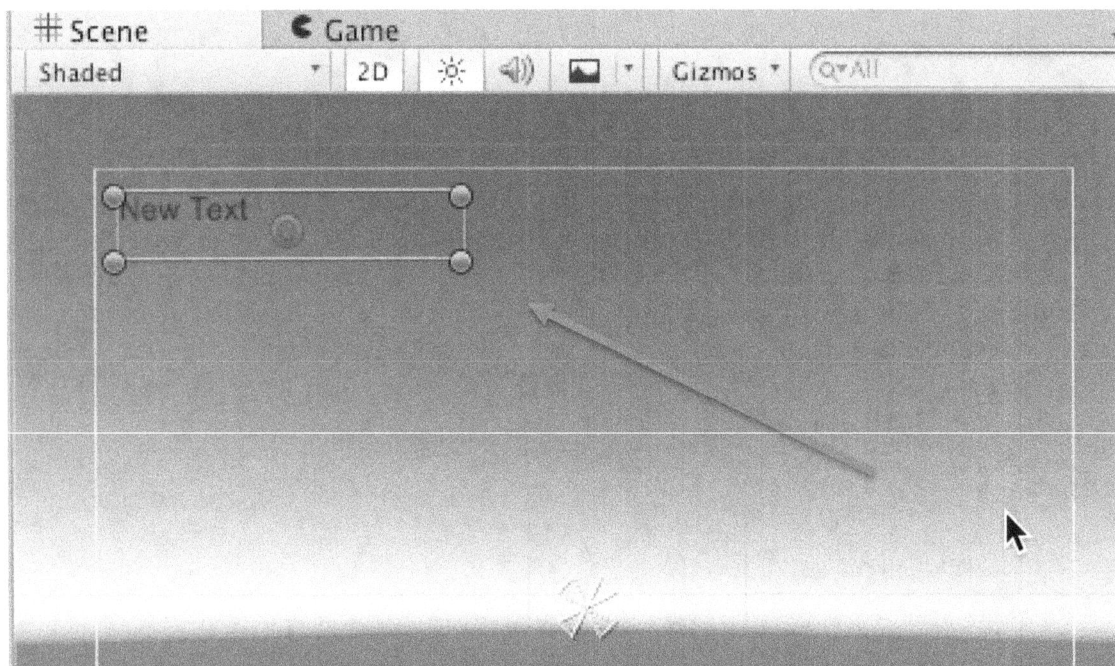

Figure 78: Adding a UI for the score

- Once this is done, you can select this object in the **Hierarchy**, duplicate it, rename the duplicate **livesUI**, and move the duplicate (i.e., **livesUI**) just below the previous **Text** object, as illustrated in the next figure.

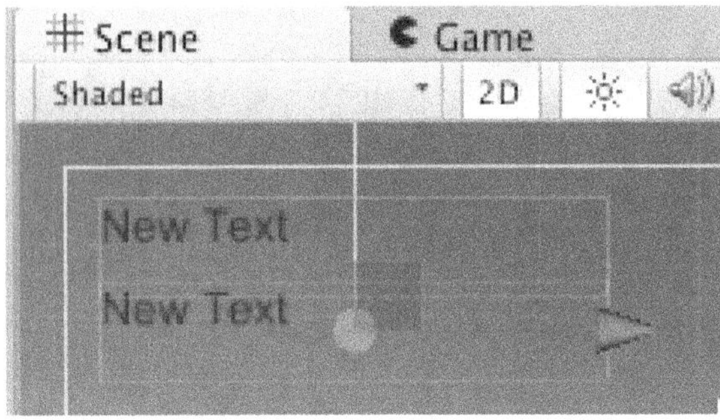

Figure 79: Adding a UI for the number of lives

- You should now have two **TextUI** elements in your **Hierarchy**: **scoreUI** and **livesUI**.

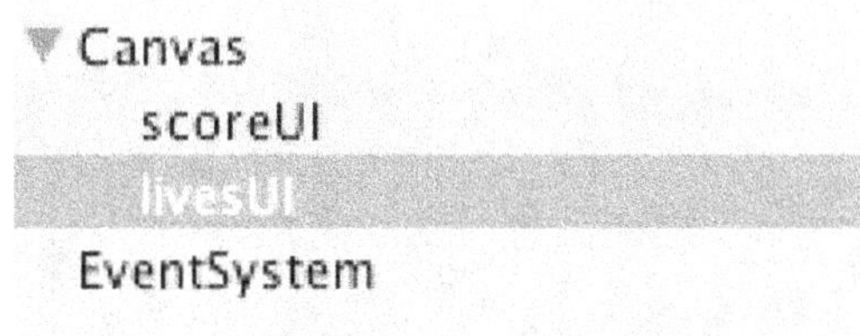

Figure 80: The two UI elements

One this is done, using the **Inspector**, you can change the font color of each of these **Text** objects, for more visibility, using their **Text Component**.

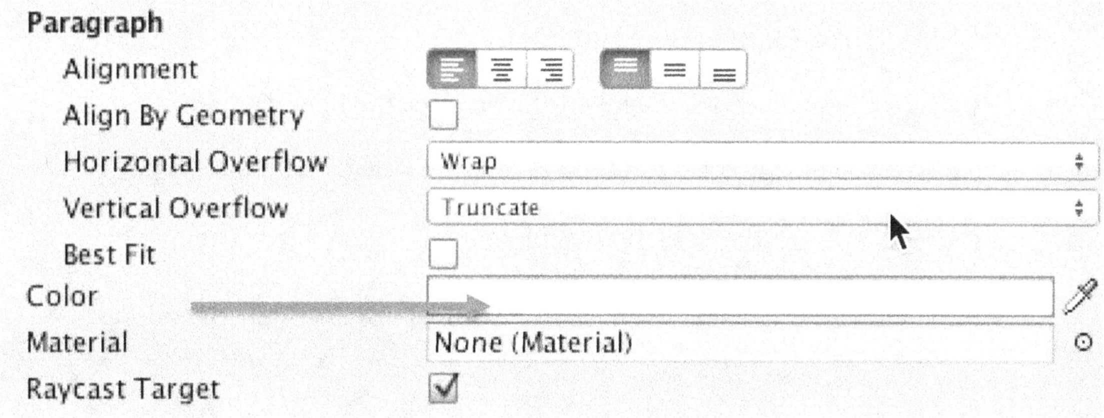

Figure 81: Changing the color of the text

Next, we need to update these text objects from our scripts, at the start of the game, and also whenever the score or the number of lives change.

- Please open the script **DetectCollision**.

- Add the following code at the beginning of the script.

```
using UnityEngine.UI;
```

- Add the following code just before the end of the script.

```
void updateUI()
{
     score = PlayerPrefs.GetInt("score");
     nbLives = PlayerPrefs.GetInt("nbLives");
     GameObject.Find("scoreUI").GetComponent<Text>().text          =
"Score: "+score;
     GameObject.Find("livesUI").GetComponent<Text>().text          =
"Lives: " +nbLives;
}
```

In the previous code:

- We create a new function called **updateUI**.

- We access the score and the number of lives from the player preferences.

- We then update the two UI objects **scoreUI** and **livesUI** with these values.

Now, we just need to initialise these **Text** fields:

- Please modify the function **Start**, in the script **DetectCollision**, as follows:

```
void Start ()
{
     updateUI ();
     nbCoinsCollectedPerLevel = 0;
}
```

In the previous code we call the function **updateUI** and also set the value of the variable **nbCoinsCollectedPerLevel** to **0**.

- Please add the following code at the end of the function **OnCollsionEnter2D**, so that the UI elements (i.e., **scoreUI** and **livesUI**) are updated after colliding with boulders or after falling.

```
updateUI();
```

- Save your script and play the scene (i.e., **level1**); you should see that the score and the number of lives are displayed at the start, and updated as you fall or when you collect items.

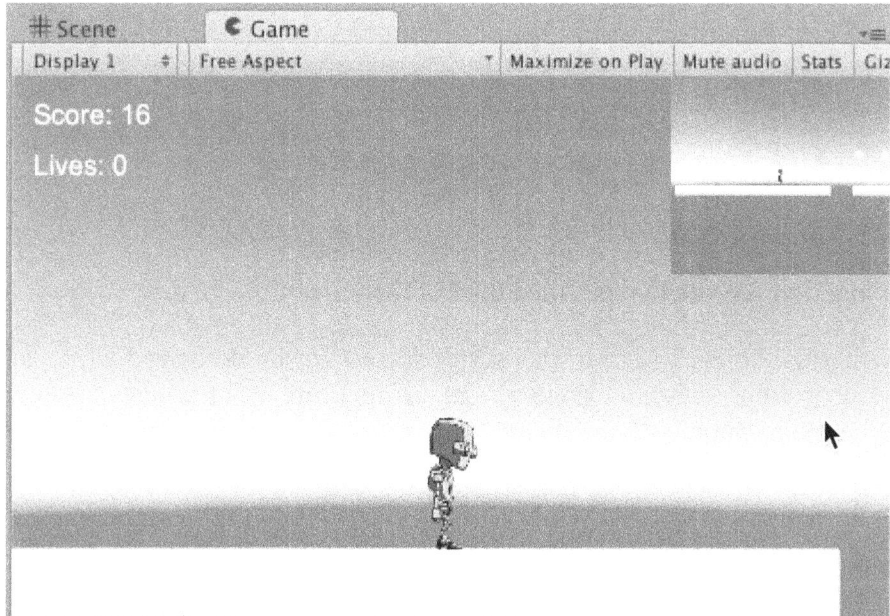

Figure 82: The UI with the score and number of lives

As you test the scene, and if you complete this level (i.e., **level1**) and proceed to the next level, you will also see that the score is not displayed in **level2**; this is because, at present, there are no UI elements added to this scene that can display this information; so we could do two things:

- Create new UI elements with the exact same name as in the first scene.

  OR

- Keep the UI elements created in the first scene.

We will opt for the second option; although the first one is also viable, the second solution decreases the workload (on the long run) as we don't have to recreate UI elements for the subsequent scenes.

So let's implement this solution.

- Create a new C# script called **KeepUI**.

- Add the following function to it.

```
void Awake()
{
    DontDestroyOnLoad(transform.gameObject);
}
```

In the previous code:

- We use the function **Awake** that is called once at the start of the game.

- We specify that the object linked to this script should not be destroyed when we load a new scene (this is usually done by default in Unity when a new scene is loaded); since this script will be linked to the canvas that includes both UI elements (**scoreUI** and **livesUI**), we make sure that these will be kept for the next scene(s).

- Please save this script, and drag and drop it on the object called **Canvas**.

- Test the scene, you should see that after completing the first scene, the second scene includes the UI elements and displays the score and the number of lives.

The only thing is that:

- When you reload the first scene (after falling) the UI is displayed twice.

- These UI elements (i.e., **scoreUI** and **livesUI**) should not be displayed in the out-of-game scenes such as the **splashScreen** or the **lose** or **win** screen; so we just need to change our code to be able to specify when these UI elements should be displayed.

So let's solve these issues one by one; first, by removing duplicate UI elements.

- Please open the scene **level1**.

- Select the object **Canvas**.

- Using the **Inspector**, create a new label called **player_ui** as we have done before.

- Apply this label to the object called **Canvas**.

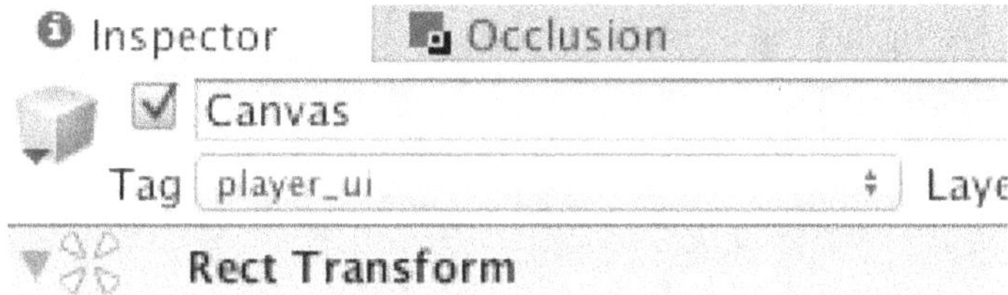

Figure 83: Setting a label for the canvas

- Once this is done, open the script called **KeepUI**.

- Add this line at the beginning of the script.

```
using UnityEngine.UI;
```

- Add this code to the function **Start**.

```
int        nbUIs       =          GameObject.FindGameObjectsWithTag
("player_ui").Length;
if (FindObjectsOfType (GetType ()).Length > 1) Destroy
(gameObject);
```

In the previous code:

- We count the number of objects with the tag **player_ui**; we effectively check whether there is more than one object called **canvas** (i.e., the object that includes the UI elements for the score and the number of lives).

- Since the function **GameObject.FindGameObjectsWithTag ("player_ui")** returns an array, **GameObject.FindGameObjectsWithTag ("player_ui").Length** will return the number of objects in this array.

- If we find a duplicate and if we are in the scene **level1** (which is bound to happen) we destroy the duplicate.

> Note that the function **GameObject.FindGameObjectsWithTag** returns an array that includes all objects with a specific tag; so using the code **GameObject.FindGameObjectsWithTag[0]** will return the first object in the array.

Last but not least, we will hide the text that is in the UI text fields whenever we are in a scene that includes a button (e.g., win, lose, or splash-screen). Now, ideally, we could use the **Start** function in the **KeepUI** script to do that; however, because this script is linked to an object that is persistent (thanks to the method **DontDesroyOnLoad**), the **Start** method will only be called in the scene **level1**; this is because it is called only when the script is loaded; however, because of the function **DontDestroyOnLoad**, the script is loaded only once (in the scene **level1**) and then kept throughout the game; so the **Start** function for the script **KeepUI** is loaded once; hence its **Start** function is only called once (throughout the game); so, for this purpose, we will use the **Start** method of an object that is loaded in the menu scenes, that is, the script called **ControlButtons**; this script is loaded every time an out-of-game scene is loaded; this means that we will be able to check whether the UI elements should be displayed every time a new scene is loaded; we will therefore be using the **Start** function of the script **ControButtons** as follows.

- Please open the script **ControButtons**.

- Add this code at the beginning of the script.

```
using UnityEngine.UI;
using UnityEngine.SceneManagement;
```

- Add this code in the **Start** function.

```
if (SceneManager.GetActiveScene ().name == "win" || currentScene
== "lose")
{
    GameObject.Find ("scoreUI").GetComponent<Text>().text = "";
    GameObject.Find ("livesUI").GetComponent<Text>().text = "";
}
```

In the previous code:

- We test whether we are in the **win** or **lose** scene.

- If this is the case, we then set the text of both UI elements to an empty string

Once this is done, we can save and use this script.

- Please save the script **ControlButtons**.

- Open the **splashScreen** scene (so that the game starts with this scene).

- Test the scene, and check that the UI elements for the score and number of lives are displayed only in the in-game scenes (i.e., **level1** and **level2**).

Finally, you can also modify the **DetectCollision** script to update the UI whenever objects are collected:

- Open the script **DetectCollison**.

- Replace the code …

```
print ("score" + score);
```

with...

```
//print ("score" + score);
updateUI();
```

You may also notice the text "**New Text**" in both UI fields at the start of each scene, as you play them; to remove this text, you can do the following:

- Open the scene **level1**.

- Select each UI elements (i.e., **uiScore** and **uiLives**).

- Using the **Inspector**, please delete the text in the **Text** Component of these objects.

Figure 84: Deleting the text in each UI Text object

- Please test the scene and check that the text "**New Text**" has disappeared.

ADDING SOUND

Ok, so far, the game runs as expected and it could be used as it is; however, we will, in this and the next sections, add some features that will make it more enjoyable and challenging. This will consist of audio clips and additional game mechanics.

We will add **Audio** components to the game in two forms: a background music that will be played in every scene, along with sound effects played when objects are collected or when the player falls.

So first let's add a background sound:

- Please import the audio tracks **Rainbows**, **On-My_Way,** and **collect_coin** from the resource pack by dragging and dropping them from their folder to the **Project** folder in Unity.

> The first two audio file were created by *Kevin McLeod* and are available on the site: http://incompetech.com/music/royalty-free/music.html; the other audio file called **collect_coin**, present in the resource folder, was created using the site http://www.bfxr.net/, which is a free tool to create your own sound effects for your game.

- You can, for the time being, create a folder called **Audio** in the **Project** window, and then add the audio files to this folder; this will make it easier to find them later.

The two first files will be used for the background music, while the last file will be used when coins have been collected.

- Please open the **splashScreen** scene.

- Create an empty object called **bg_sound** (select **GameObject | Create Empty**).

- Drag and drop the audio file **On_My_Way** on this empty object; this will create an **Audio Source** component for this object with the option **playOnAwake** set to **true** by default.

- Please select the empty object **bg_sound**, and, using the **Inspector** view, set the attribute **Loop** for the component **Audio Source**, to **true**.

Figure 85: Setting the attributes of the background sound

- Once this is done, you can play the scene and check that the background sound is played.

When you have checked that it is working, you can repeat the last steps to add the same background sound to the scenes **win**, and **lose**, and the background sound called **Rainbows** to the scenes **level1** and **level2**.

Once this is done, please check that the background music plays as expected; you can, of course, use other types of background sounds of your choice if you wish, using **wav** or **mp3** files, for example.

Next, we will add sound effects when objects are collected.

- Please open the scene **level1**.

- Select the object **player** in the **Hierarchy**.

- From the top menu, select **Component | Audio | Audio Source**; this will add an **Audio Source** component to your object;

Whenever you need to play a sound, an **Audio Source** is needed, and it is comparable to an mp3 player in the sense that it plays audio clips that you need to select, the same way you would select a particular track on your mp3 player (hoping mp3 player are still popular when this book comes out :-)).

- Please, drag and drop the audio file called **collect_coin** from the **Project** window to the **Audio Clip** attribute of the **Audio Source** and set the attribute **Play on Awake** to **false** (i.e., unchecked) so that this sound is not played automatically at the start of the scene, as illustrated on the next figure.

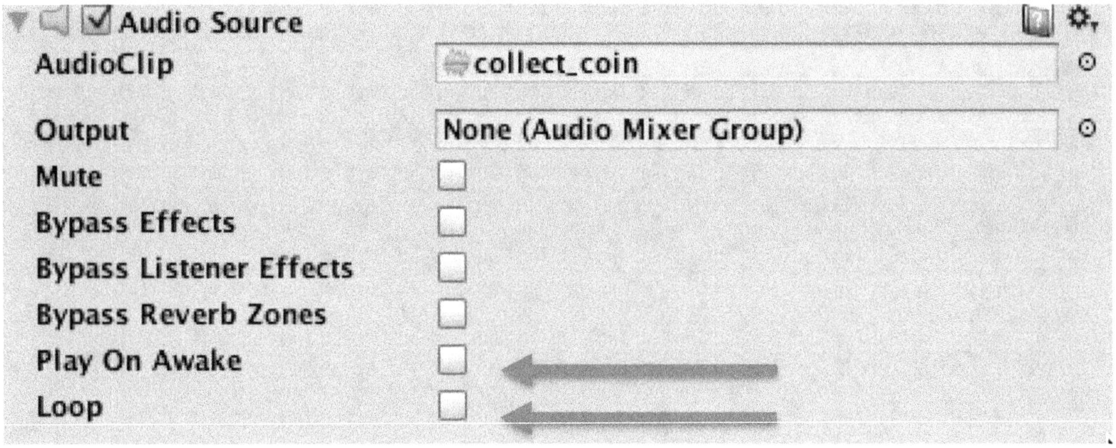

Figure 86: Setting the attributes of the sound effect

Next, we will write code that will access this **Audio Source** and play the clip, whenever we collect an object.

- Please open the script called **DetectCollision**.

- Add the following code to the function **OnCollisionEnter2D** (new cold in bold).

```
if (tag == "pick_me")
{
        GetComponent<AudioSource> ().Play ();
```

In the previous code, we access the **AudioSource** component that is linked to the object **player** (i.e., the object linked to this script), and we play the clip that is included in this **AudioSource** (i.e., **collect_coins**).

- Please save your code, test the scene, and check that the audio clip is played whenever you collect an object.

PLAYING MULTIPLE SOUNDS

As you know, feedback is very important in video games, as it provides additional information to the users on their progress; using audio is one of the many ways to provide feedback and to make sure that the experience is entertaining and interactive.

Since we are adding audio for collecting coins, we could also add audio when the user has made a wrong move; this is, again, for feedback.

Now, because the **Audio Source** will need to play several sounds (a different sound depending on whether the player collects a coin or hits a boulder), we will need to specify which track needs to be played, so we will modify our script accordingly.

- Please import the audio file called **hurt.wav** from the resource pack (i.e., drag and drop this file to the **Project** window).

Figure 87: Importing the hurt.wav audio file

- Please open the script **DetectCollision**.

- Add the following lines at the beginning of the script:

```
public AudioClip collect, hurt;
```

- This code declares two audio clips; because they are public, they will be accessible from the **Inspector**, and as a result, we will be able to set (or initialize) these variables by dragging and dropping objects to their placeholders in the Inspector window.

- Please save your script, switch to Unity, select the **player** object and display the **Inspector** window.

- You should see that two variables, that act as placeholders, are now available.

Figure 88: Initializing the audio clips (part1)

- Please drag and drop the sound **hurt.wav** from the **Project** view, to the variable **hurt** in the **Inspector**, and the sound **collect_coin** from the **Project** view to the variable **collect** in the **Inspector** view, as illustrated in the next figure.

Figure 89: Initializing the audio clips (part 2)

Now, it's time to modify the script further to tell the system which audio clip to play and when.

- Please open the script **DetectCollision**.

- Add the following code (new code in bold):

```
if (tag == "pick_me)
{
        GetComponent<AudioSource> ().clip = collect;
        GetComponent<AudioSource> ().Play ();
```

In the previous code:

- We specify that the new clip to be played is the clip called **collect** (which contains the audio **collect-coin.wav**); this track is now the default track for the **Audio Source**.

- We then play the track that we have selected.

We will also use similar code to play a different sound when the player is hurt.

- Please add the following code in the function **OnCollisionEnter2D** (new code in bold).

```
if (tag == "avoid_me" || tag == "reStarter")
{
        GetComponent<AudioSource> ().clip = hurt;
        GetComponent<AudioSource> ().Play ();
```

In the previous code, following the same principle, we select the clip that contains the audio file **hurt.wav** and we then play this clip.

- You can now save your script and test the scene **level1**;

- You should hear a different sound every time you collect an object or collide with a boulder.

Now, this code works well in the first level, however, we may obtain an error message after progressing to the second level whenever you collide with a coin; the message may read "**There is no Audio Source attached to the player**"; this is because the player that we are using in **level2** is different to the one used in **level1** as it has no **AudioSource** component yet; to avoid this issue, we will update our **player** prefab in the scene **level1** (so that the prefab for the **player** object includes an **Audio Source**) and then use the same prefab in the scene **level2** (or any other subsequent in-game scene).

- Please open the scene **level1**.

- Select the object called **player**.

- Using the **Inspector**, click on the button called **Apply**, as illustrated on the next figure.

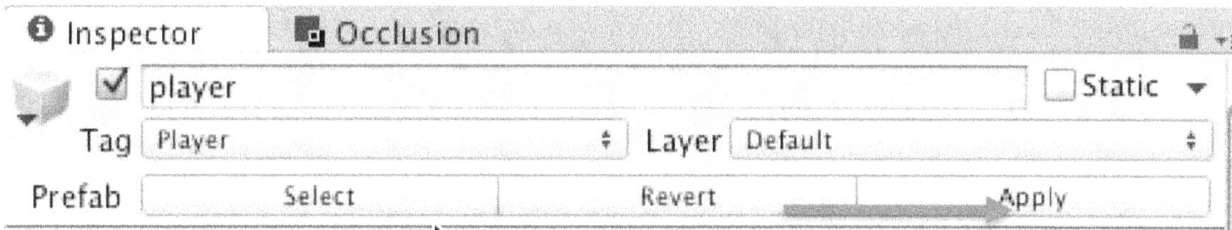

Figure 90: Applying changes to the player prefab

- This will apply the changes to the **player** prefab; and since **level2** includes a player based on the same prefab, the error mentioned earlier should now disappear if we play the game again.

- Please play the second scene and check that the error has disappeared.

LEVEL ROUNDUP

Summary

In this chapter, we have managed to use the player preferences to store information that is now accessible throughout the level; we also created a mechanism by which the UI for the score and the number of lives is created only once but displayed in every in-game scene. Finally, we also learned to import and to play sounds either as a background music or as a sound effect.

Checklist

You can consider moving to the next stage if you can do the following:

- Understand when the function **Awake** is called.

- Understand how to create and access variables stored in the player preferences.

- Understand the difference between the components **Audio Clip** and **Audio Source**.

Quiz

Now, let's check your knowledge! Please answer the following questions (the answers are included in the resource pack) or specify whether they are correct or incorrect.

1. It is possible to store integers, Booleans or strings in the player preferences.

2. The following code will create a new variable called **score** in the player preferences.

```
PlayerPrefs.SetInt("score",10);
```

3. The following code will read a variable called **score** from the player preferences.

```
int s = PlayerPrefs.ReadInt("score");
```

4. Provided that this code is attached to an object with an **Audio Source** component, it will play its default clip.

```
GetCOmponent<AudioSource>().Play();
```

5. In Unity, it is possible to play several **Audio Clips** using just one **Audio Source**.

6. By default, the attribute **Play on Awake** for an **Audio Clip** is set to true.

7. By default, the attribute **Loop** for an **Audio Clip** is set to true.

8. The following code, when attached to an object, will ensure that it is not destroyed when the next scene loads.

```
void Awake()
{
    DontDestroyOnLoad(transform.gameObject);
}
```

9. For a particular script, the function **Start** is called when the script is loaded.

10. For a particular script, the function **Start** is called <u>only</u> when the game is loaded.

Challenge 1

For this chapter, your challenge will be to mute the sound when the player presses the key **M**, and you could do as follows:

- Detect when the key **M** has been pressed; you can use the following code in the **Update** function:

```
If (Input.GetKeyDown(KeyCode.M)) {}
```

- Whenever this happens, access the **Audio Source** attached to this object.
- Then, access the **mute** option of the audio source using the following code, and set it to **true** or **false,** or to the opposite of the current value using the operator **!**:

```
GetComponent<AudioSource>.mute
```

For more information about the mute attribute, you can look at the official documentation using the following link:

https://docs.unity3d.com/ScriptReference/AudioSource-mute.html

4

ADDING CHALLENGING GAMEPLAY

In this section, we will start to include game mechanics that improve the gameplay for the platform game that we have been creating so far; after completing this chapter, you will be able to:

- Create moving platforms.

- Create a shaky bridge for which the steps fall down as you walk on them.

- Create a timer.

- Teleport the character.

Some of the skills you will learn in the process include:

- Using **Time.deltaTime**.

- Enabling or disabling gravity for **Rigidbody2D** components.

- Animate objects.

INTRODUCTION

At present, the scenes that we have created include some simple game mechanics that may challenge the player; however, as you will expand your game, it is always a good idea to change and vary the types of challenges that the player has to overcome; so, in the next sections, we will create a series of game mechanics or challenges, that you will be able to save as prefabs and to reuse in any level of your choice; these will consist of:

- **A time challenge**: the player has to complete the level before the time is up.

- **Moving platforms**: these include platforms moving horizontally or vertically.

- **A shaky Bridge**: a bridge for which the steps progressively fall as the player walks on them, forcing the player to keep moving forward, and fast.

- **Magic doors (i.e., teleportation)**: this consists of a door that teleports the player to a different part of the game when reached by the player.

THE TIME CHALLENGE

So, let's start with the time challenge, it will consist of a timer that counts down from 30 seconds; whenever the timer reaches 0, the player loses a life and the level needs to be restarted; the time is displayed onscreen.

So let's get started:

- Please open the first scene (**level1**).

- Create an empty object, and rename it **timer**.

- Create a new C# script (from the **Project** window, select **Create | C# Script**).

- Rename this script **Timer**.

- Add the following code at the beginning of the script.

```
using UnityEngine.SceneManagement;
```

- Add the following code at the beginning of the class.

```
float timer;
int seconds;
```

In the previous code

- We declare a variable called **timer** that will be used to calculate the time; it is declared as a **float**.
- We also declare an **integer** variable called **seconds** (used to store the number of seconds remaining).

- Please modify the **Start** function as follows:

```
void Start ()
{
    timer = 30;
    seconds = 0;
}
```

- In the previous, code we initialize the variable **timer** to **30** and the number of seconds elapsed to **0**.

- Please modify the function **Update** as follows:

```
void Update ()
{
    timer -= Time.deltaTime;
    seconds = (int) (timer);
    print ("Seconds"+seconds);
    if (seconds <= 0)
    {
        int nbLives = PlayerPrefs.GetInt("nbLives");
        nbLives--;
        PlayerPrefs.SetInt("nbLives", nbLives);
        if                  (nbLives                >=                0)
SceneManager.LoadScene(SceneManager.GetActiveScene().name);
        else SceneManager.LoadScene("lose");
    }
}
```

In the previous code:

- We use the variable **Time.deltaTime** to update the variable **timer**; **Time.deltaTime** is the number of seconds elapsed since the last frame; so it effectively returns the number of seconds, regardless of the computer where the game is played; this solves any possible issue (or differences) linked to frame rate, so that the time is consistent across players.

- We decrease the value of the variable **timer**.

- We then convert the **timer** from a **float** type to an **integer**; this is because we don't need the decimals values; this will also be useful if we want to display the time onscreen without the decimals.

- We then check for the value of the variable **seconds**.

- If it is **0** or less (i.e., if the time is up) we update the number of lives and restart the current level or load the scene called **lose**.

That's it!

You can now drag and drop the script **Timer** to the object **timer** and play the scene; please check that you can see the time displayed in the **Console** window and that the scene restarts if the time is up.

You may notice that the last part of the code is identical to the code included in the script **DetectCollision**; in fact, it is an exact copy/paste from it:

```
int nbLives = PlayerPrefs.GetInt("nbLives");
nbLives--;
PlayerPrefs.SetInt("nbLives", nbLives);
if                     (nbLives                 >=                 0)
SceneManager.LoadScene(SceneManager.GetActiveScene().name);
else SceneManager.LoadScene("lose");
```

So what we could do, instead of repeating this code, and also to have it in only one place (i.e., this is neater and more practical), is the following:

- Create a function in the script **DetectCollsion**, that executes this code.

- Call this function from the script **Timer** when needed.

So let's do just that:

- Please open the script called **DetectCollision**.

- Locate the following code.

```
int nbLives = PlayerPrefs.GetInt("nbLives");
nbLives--;
PlayerPrefs.SetInt("nbLives", nbLives);
if                     (nbLives                 >=                 0)
SceneManager.LoadScene(SceneManager.GetActiveScene().name);
else SceneManager.LoadScene("lose");
```

- Cut (*CTRL + C*) this code.

- Type the following code exactly where you removed the previous code (new code in bold).

```
if (tag == "avoid_me" || tag == "reStarter")
{
        DecreaseLives ();
        GetComponent<AudioSource> ().clip = hurt;
        GetComponent<AudioSource> ().Play ();
```

- Then create a new function in the same script, and called **DecreaseLives**.

- Paste the code that you have just copied inside this function.

```
public void DecreaseLives()
{
     int nbLives = PlayerPrefs.GetInt ("nbLives");
     nbLives--;
     PlayerPrefs.SetInt ("nbLives", nbLives);
     if (nbLives >= 0)
          SceneManager.LoadScene     (SceneManager.GetActiveScene
().name);
     else
          SceneManager.LoadScene ("lose");
}
```

Note that this function is public, so it is accessible from outside the class **DetectCollision**; this is important as we will need to access it from the script called **Timer**.

Finally, we can now call this function from the script **Timer**.

- Please open the script called **Timer**.

- Replace this code….

```
if (seconds <= 0)
{
     int nbLives = PlayerPrefs.GetInt("nbLives");
     nbLives--;
     PlayerPrefs.SetInt("nbLives", nbLives);
     if              (nbLives              >=              0)
SceneManager.LoadScene(SceneManager.GetActiveScene().name);
     else SceneManager.LoadScene("lose");

}
```

with this code…

```
if (seconds <= 0)
{
    GameObject.Find       ("player").GetComponent<DetectCollision>
().DecreaseLives ();
}
```

In the previous code, we access the function called **DecreaseLives**, from the script called **DetectCollosion**, that is attached to the object **player**.

That's it.

- Please save both scripts (**DetectCollision** and **Timer**) and test the game.

- Check the time in the **Console** window, and that when it has elapsed the player restarts the level or the scene called **lose** is played.

The last thing we need for this game mechanic is to display the time onscreen; so we will use **UI** elements.

- Please open the scene **level1**, and duplicate the object **livesUI** (that is a child of the object called **canvas**).

- Rename it **timerUI**.

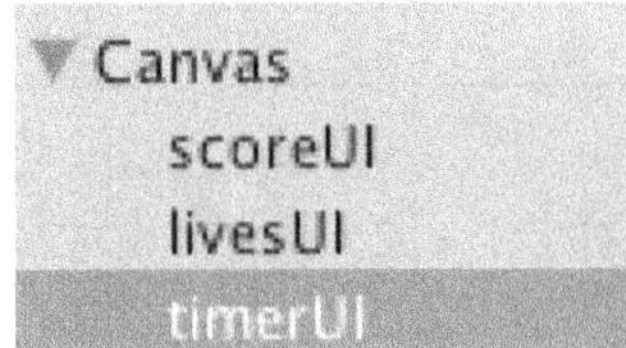

Figure 91: Creating a UI object for the timer

Once this is done, it is time to update the content of the **timerUI** object from our **Timer** script.

- Please open the script called **Timer**.

- Add the following code to the beginning of the script.

```
using UnityEngine.UI;
```

- In the **Udpate** function, replace the code

```
print ("Seconds"+seconds);
```

with...

```
GameObject.Find ("timerUI").GetComponent<Text> ().text = "time: "
+ seconds;
```

- In the previous code, we set the text of the UI Text component to include the message "time: " followed by the time in seconds.

- Please save your script.

Last but not least, so that the timer does not appear on the menu scenes, we just need to modify the script called **ControlButtons**.

- Please open the script **ControlButtons**.

- Add the following line to the **Start** function (new code in bold).

```
GameObject.Find ("scoreUI").GetComponent<Text>().text = "";
GameObject.Find ("livesUI").GetComponent<Text>().text = "";
GameObject.Find ("timerUI").GetComponent<Text>().text = "";
```

- Please save your script and test the scene.

That's it; so our time is working fairly well; we just need to make a prefab from it so that it can be reused in other scenes:

- Please drag and drop the object called **timer** from the **Hierarchy** to the **Project** window.

- This will create a prefab called **timer**.

Figure 92: Creating a timer prefab

You can now keep the object called timer in the **Hierarchy** or deleted it to use it only in other levels.

CREATING MOVING PLATFORMS.

Moving platforms are also great gameplay elements; they are challenging as the player needs to adjust the timing of the jump to the changing position of the platform. So, in this section:

- We will create both horizontal and vertical platforms.

- Each of these platforms will move forth and back or up and down from their initial position; we will also ensure that the player, once s/he has reached the platform, sticks to it, until s/he jumps again.

- We will then create prefabs from these platforms so that they can be reused in different scenes.

So let's create these platforms.

- Please open the scene **level2**.

As you can see on the next figure, it consists of simple static platforms; so we will modify some of these so that they start moving indefinitely.

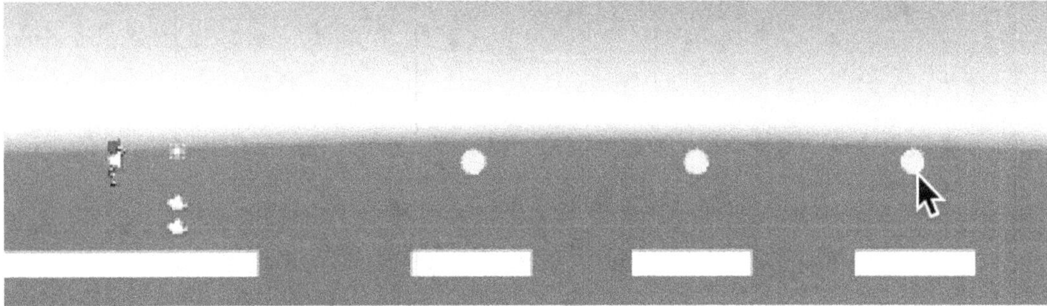

Figure 93: An overview of level2

- Please select the first small platform (the closest to the character), as indicated in the next figure.

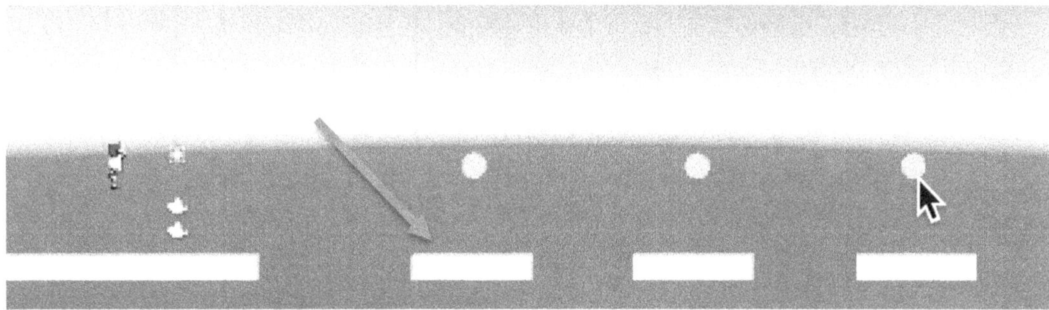

Figure 94: An overview of level2

- Drag and drop it (the small platform) to the **Project** view, to create a new prefab.

- Call this prefab **moving_platform_horizontal**.

- Delete the first small platform in the **Scene** view (i.e., the platform that was used to create the prefab).

- Drag and drop the prefab **moving_platform_horizontal** at the same location.

You should now have an object called **moving_platform_horizontal** in the **Hierarchy**, and we will now create a script that will manage the movement of this platform.

- Please create a new C# script named **MovingPlatformHorizontal**.

- Open this script.

- Add the following code to it (new code in bold).

```
float timer, direction;
void Start ()
{
        direction = 0.1f;
}
```

In the previous code:

- We declare a variable **timer**, used to time the movement of the platform, as well as a variable called **direction** that will be used to set the direction of the platform (i.e., left or right).

- We then initialize the direction; **1** will be for **right** and **-1** will be for **left**; so initially, the platform will be moving to the right.

- Please add the following code (new code in bold):

```
void Update ()
{
    timer += Time.deltaTime;
    transform.Translate (Vector3.right * direction);
    if (timer >= 1)
    {
        direction *= -1;
        timer = 0;
    }
}
```

In the previous code:

- We use a timer, as we have done in the past; this timer will tick and once it reaches 1 (i.e., one second), we will then change the direction of the platform (to the opposite direction using **-1**).

- We set the direction of the platform to the right (**Vector3.right** multiplied by one).

- If the timer reaches **1** then we change the variable direction to **-1**; this will result in changing the overall direction to its opposite (i.e., **left**), and we then initialize the timer again.

- Please save the script and check that it is error-free.

Once this is done, we can attach this script to the object **moving_platform_horizontal**:

- Please drag and drop the script called **moving_platform_horizontal** from the **Project** window to the object called **moving_platform_horizontal** in the **Hierarchy**.

- Select the object **moving_platform_horizontal** and click on the button **Apply** (in the **Inspector**), to apply the changes to the corresponding prefab.

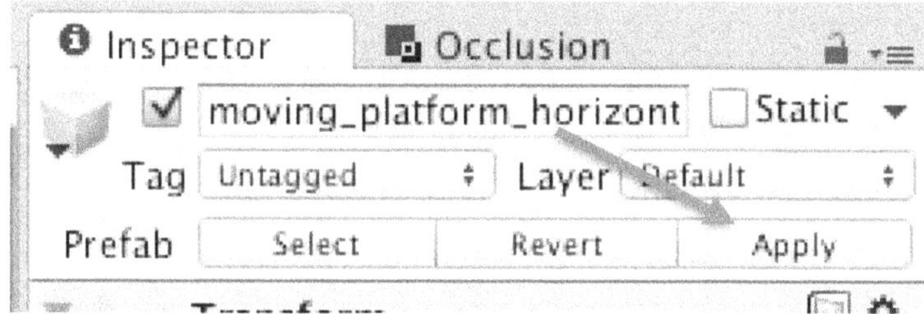

Figure 95: Applying changes to the prefab

- Please play the scene and check that the platform is moving.

As you play the scene, you may also notice that when you are moving on the platform, the character slides on it; so, while this could be an extra challenge, we could, for the time being improve this behaviour so that the player, just after landing on the platform, does not slide (i.e., so that it sticks to it).

- Please select the object called **moving_platform_horizontal** in the **Hierarchy**.

- Create a new tag called **moving_platform** and apply it to this object.

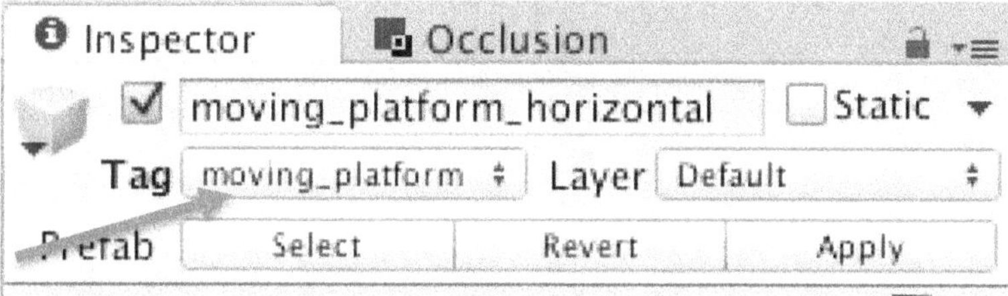

Figure 96: Applying a new tag

- Once this is done, please open the script **DetectCollision**.

- Add this code at the beginning of the class.

```
bool isOnMovingPlatform = false;
```

- This variable will be used to check whether we are on the moving platform.

- Please add the following code to the function **OnCollisionEnter2D**.

```
if (tag == "moving_platform")
{
    transform.parent = coll.gameObject.transform;
    isOnMovingPlatform = true;
}
```

- In the previous code, if we collide with the moving platform (i.e., the object with the tag **moving_platform**), then the player becomes a child of this object; this means that any movement applied to the platform (e.g., translating to the right or left) will also be applied to the player.

- We also set the variable **isOnMovingPlatform** to **true**.

- You can save your script and test the scene; you will see that when the player jumps on the platforms, it will, without any further action from the payer, move with the platform.

Figure 97: The player moving with the platform

This being said, if you try to jump again from the platform, the movement will not be smooth and it will be difficult to reach the other edge; this is because your movement is then calculated based on the platform which is now the parent of the player; so to remove this issue, we can, specify that the platform is no longer a parent of the **player** object when the player jumps from (or off) the platform;

- Please open the script **DetectCollision**.

- Add the following function.

```
void OnCollisionExit2D (Collision2D coll)
{
    if (isOnMovingPlatform)
    {
        transform.parent = null;
        isOnMovingPlatform = false;
    }
}
```

In the previous code:

- We use the function **OnCollisionExit2D** which is called when the player is exiting a collision with an object; in our case, whenever s/he jumps off the platform.

- In this case we specify that the platform is no longer its parent, using the **null** object.

- We also set the variable **isOnMovingPlatform** to **false**.

That's it!

- Please save your code and test the scene again.

Note: you may notice errors in the **Console** window saying "**Object reference not set..**"; this is because the script **DetectCollision** is looking for one of the **UI** elements that is not present in the scene yet; these elements would usually be created in **level1** and then kept (remember, the score and live UI objects are created in the first scene and then kept); so you may ignore these messages for the time being, as you are testing this scene independently.

So that is working well; we can now update and save our moving platform prefab.

- Select the object **moving_platform_horizontal** and, using the **Inspector**, click on the button **Apply**, located in the top-right corner of the **Inspector** window, to apply the changes to the corresponding prefab.

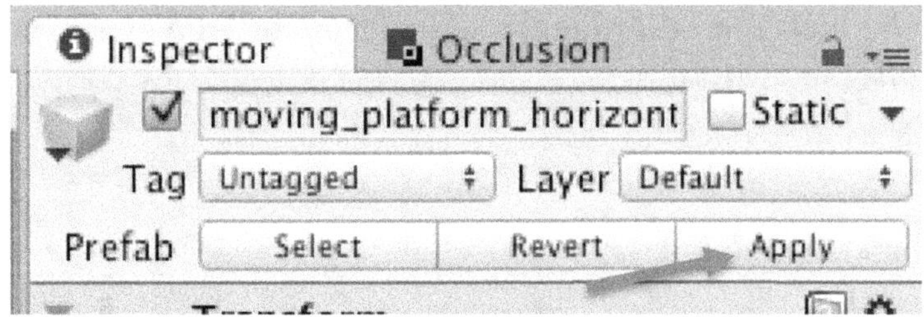

Figure 98: Applying changes to the prefab

Last but not least, we could create moving platforms that move, this time, vertically, just like an escalator. The principle will be the exact same as what we have done so far, except that the movement will be using the up and down directions. For this we will duplicate both the prefab and the script used for the horizontal moving platform and modify these slightly.

- Using the **Project** window, please duplicate the prefab called **moving_platform_horizontal**, and rename it **moving_platform_vertical**.

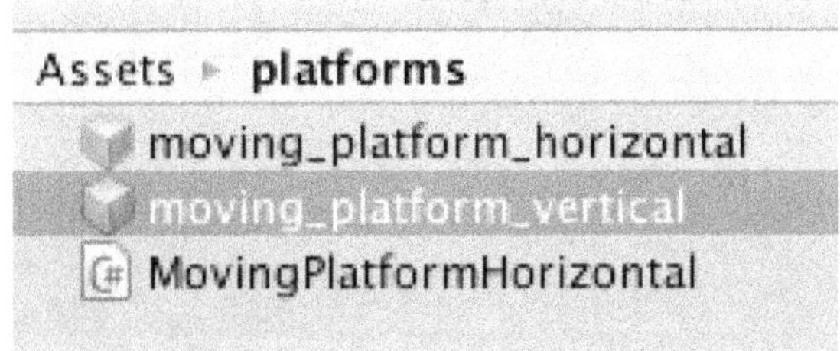

Figure 99: Duplicating the platform prefab

- Duplicate the script **MovingPlatformHorizontal** and rename it **MovingPlatformVertical**.

- As you do so, Unity may let you know of an error; this is because the name of the new script (**MovingPlatformVertical**) does not match the name of the class inside this script (**MovingPlatformHorizontal**).

- Please open the script **MovingPlatformVertical** and modify the first line as follows.

- Change this code…

```
public class MovingPlatformHorizontal: MonoBehaviour {
```

to…

```
public class MovingPlatformVertical : MonoBehaviour {
```

This will remove the error due to the clash between the name of the class and the name of the script.

We can now change the movement of the platform:

- Please change the line…

```
transform.Translate (Vector3.right * direction);
```

to …

```
transform.Translate (Vector3.up * direction);
```

- You can now save the script.

We just need to link this new script to the corresponding prefab.

- Please select the prefab **moving_platform_vertical** from the **Project** window.

- Using the **Inspector** window, remove the script component **MovingPlatformHorizontal** from this prefab: right-click on the component **MovingPlatformHorizontal**, and select **Remove Component**.

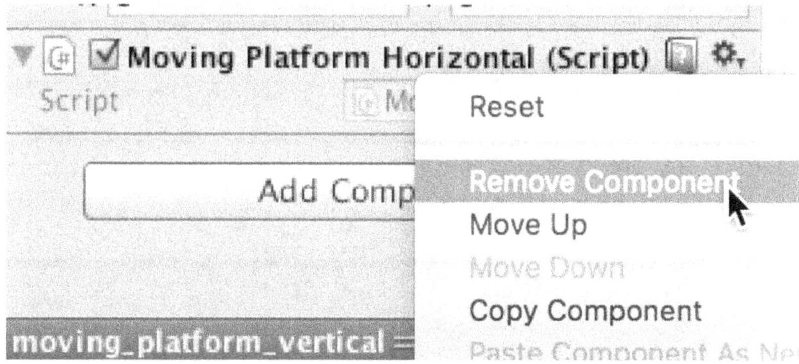

Figure 100: Removing the previous script component

- Now that the previous script has been removed, please drag and drop the script **MovingPlatformVertical** to this object from the **Project** window; this will create a new script component called **MovingPlatformVertical**, as illustrated on the next figure.

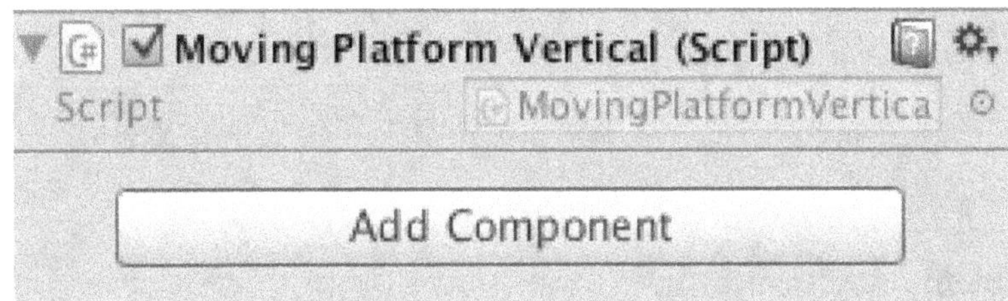

Figure 101: Adding a new script

- Once this is done, we can drag and drop the prefab **moving_platform_vertical** to the **Scene** view; this will create a new object called **moving_platform_vertical** in the **Hierarchy**.

- Please save your scene and test it; you should see both the horizontal and vertical platforms moving at the same time.

Note that you can use and modify this game mechanic to create a moving character from left to right. In this case, every time you change the direction of this character, you can also flip the image horizontally, so that the image matches the direction where this character is going. This can be achieved using **GetComponent<SpriteRenderer>().flipX.** For more information on this function, you can check the official documentation on the following page:

https://docs.unity3d.com/ScriptReference/SpriteRenderer-flipX.html

Using this same game mechanic, you could also create two spikes moving vertically, one moving up and one moving down at the same time; these could be made of triangles, for example.

CREATING MAGIC DOORS

So our platforms are working well, and it would be great to add another interesting gameplay element called **magic door**; put simply, if you collide with (or walk through) a special object, your player will be teleported to a different part of the level.

Let's create this feature:

- Please open the first level (**level1**).

- Create a new sprite (i.e., square), using the **Project** window (**Create | Sprites | Square**), and rename it **door**.

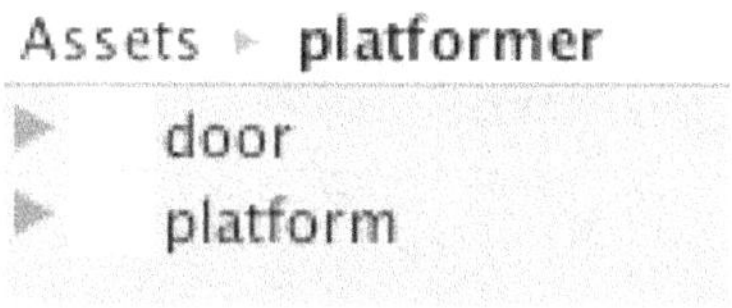

Assets ▸ **platformer**
▸ door
▸ platform

Figure 102: Creating a new sprite

- Once this is done, you can drag and drop this asset to the scene, it will create an object called **door**.

- Please rename this new object **magic_door_entrance**.

- Duplicate this object and rename the duplicate **magic_door_exit**.

- Move the first one (i.e., the object **magic_door_entrance**) just before the boulders and the second one just after the boulders; the idea will be that the player will be able to avoid going through the boulders by just entering the magic door, as described on the next figure.

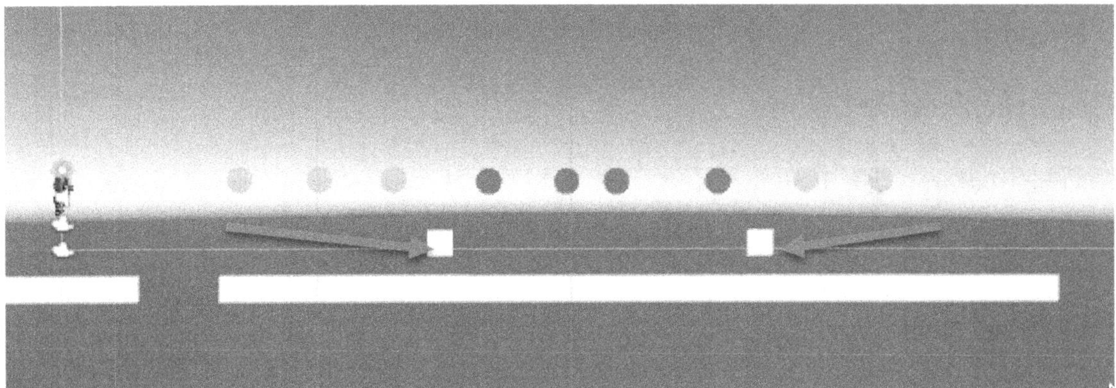

Figure 103: Adding the magic entrance

Once this is done, we will modify the properties of these objects:

- Please select the object **magic_door_entrance** in the **Hierarchy**.

- Add a **Box Collider2D** to it: select **Component | Physics2D | Box Collider2D**.

- Using the **Inspector**, modify the attribute **Is Triger** to true for the component **Box Collider2D** for this object.

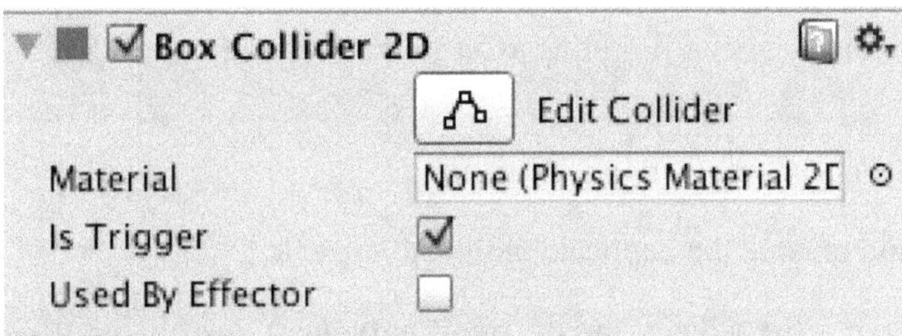

Figure 104: Setting the collider as a trigger

So, what is the difference between a trigger and a collider?

Well, when a collider is added to an object, it will collide with the other objects; in this case, the function **OnCollisionEnter2D** will be called; however, when the attribute called **Is Trigger** is set to true, this object becomes a trigger; this means that the object no longer has the ability to collide with other objects; however, its shape is used to define a space that is used as a trigger; in other words, by entering this space the trigger is set (i.e., we detect that an object has entered this area); in this case, the function **OnTriggerEnter2D** is called instead.

Next, we will make sure that the exit is not visible, as we just want the player to be teleported to the location defined by the object **magic_door_exit**.

- Please select the object called **magic_door_exit**.

- Using the **Inspector** window, please deactivate its **Sprite Renderer** component (i.e., for the object **magic_door_entrance**).

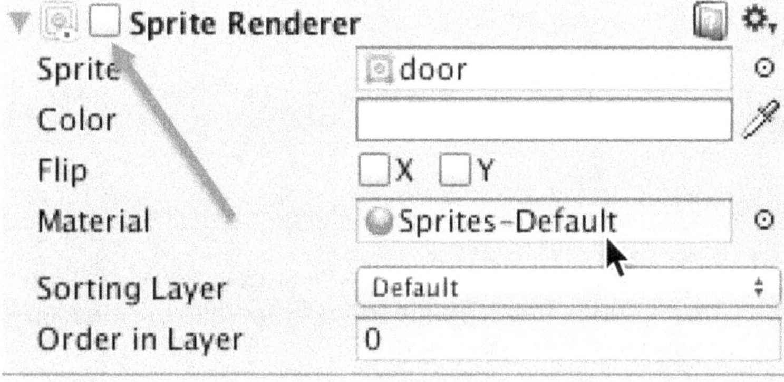

Figure 105: Deactivating the Sprite Renderer

Once this is done, we can then modify the code in the script called **DetectCollision**, so that our player is **teleported** to the second door upon entering the trigger defined by the first one.

- Please open the script **DetectCollision**, and add the following function:

```
void OnTriggerEnter2D(Collider2D coll)
{
     if (coll.gameObject.name == "magic_door_entrance")
     {
          transform.position          =          GameObject.Find
("magic_door_exit").transform.position;
     }
}
```

In the previous code:

- We use the function **OnTriggerEnter2D**.

- We check for the name of the trigger that we are entering.

- If it is the **entrance**, we then move our player to the position of the **exit**.

Please save this script and test the scene. As the character walks through the entrance, it will then appear directly at the exit.

Once you have checked that the magic doors are working, we can create a prefab accordingly by doing the following:

- Create an empty object called **magic_doors**.

- Using the **Hierarchy** window, drag and drop the objects **magic_door_entrance** and **magic_door_exit** on the empty object **magic_doors**, so that they become children of this object, as illustrated on the next figure.

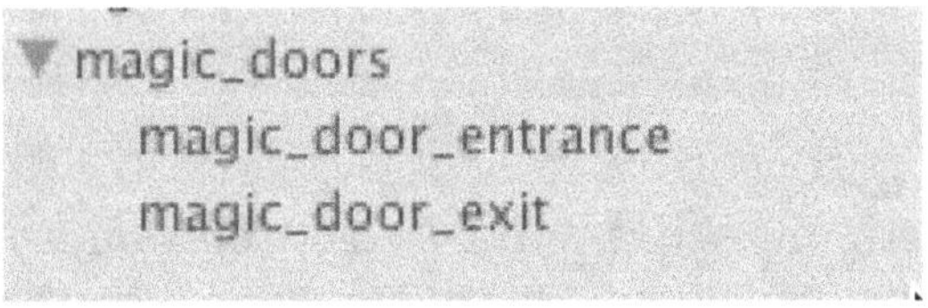

▼ magic_doors
    magic_door_entrance
    magic_door_exit

Figure 106: Grouping the two doors

- We can then drag and drop the object called **magic_doors** to the **Project** window, to create a corresponding prefab that can be used in other scenes.

Figure 107: Creating a prefab for the doors

Note that, when reusing this prefab, you can move each door separately to different locations to match your level and design.

CREATING A SHAKY BRIDGE

In this section, we will create a shaky bridge, a bridge that collapses as the player walks on it. For this, we will reuse the **small_platform** prefab and modify it by adding a **Rigidbody2D** component to it. We will then either activate or deactivate the gravity on this object so that it starts to fall only when the player collides with it.

So let's get started:

- Please duplicate the scene **level2**: in the **Project** window, select the scene **level2** and then press *CTRL + D (or APPLE + D)*.

- This will create a new scene called **scene3**.

- Remove all the objects present in the scene except from the player, the mini-camera, and the platform that is underneath the player.

- In the **Project** window, locate the prefab called **small_platform** (to make things easier, you can use the search window located in the **Project** view).

- Duplicate the prefab **small_platform** and rename the duplicate **shaky_step**.

- Drag and drop this new prefab (**shaky_step**) to the **Scene** view three times to create three steps as per the next figure.

Figure 108: Creating more steps

Once this is done, we will modify these objects:

- Please select thee three steps in the **Hierarchy**.

Note that you can select several objects by pressing the *CTRL* key, as you click on these items individually in the **Hierarchy**.

- From the top menu, select **Component | Physics2D | RigidBody2D**; this will add a **Rigidbody** component to these objects so that they can fall (i.e., subject to gravity).

Once this is done, we just need to make sure that these start to fall only when the player collides with them.

- Please create a new C# script called **ShakyStep**.

- Add the following code to it (new code in bold).

```
void Start () {
    GetComponent<Rigidbody2D> ().isKinematic = true;
}
void Update () {

}
void OnCollisionEnter2D (Collision2D coll)
{
    GetComponent<Rigidbody2D> ().isKinematic = false;
    Destroy (gameObject, 3.0f);
}
```

In the previous code:

- In the **Start** function, we access the **Rigidbody2D** component of the object linked to the script (this will be the shaky step), and we set the variable **isKinematic** to true; this will have the effects of keeping the object in place (i.e., removing gravity) for the time-being.

- Then, whenever a collision is detected (we assume that only the player will collide with these steps, but we could also have checked for the name of the object colliding with the step), we set the variable **isKinematic** to false, so that the step can start to fall; we also destroy the step after 3 seconds.

We can now save our script and prefab:

- Please save this script and drag and drop it on all the three steps.

- You can also update the corresponding prefab by selecting one of these steps and by then clicking on the button called **Apply** located in the top right corner of the **Inspector**.

- After this, you can test the scene and check that the steps fall when the player jumps on them.

Figure 109: Falling step from the bridge

Once we know that this is working, we could also create a prefab called **shaky_bridge** that includes a series of 10 shaky steps; again, this will make future levels creation much easier.

- Please duplicate one of the shaky steps seven times and arrange all the steps so that the 10 steps form a bridge, with some small gaps between the steps.

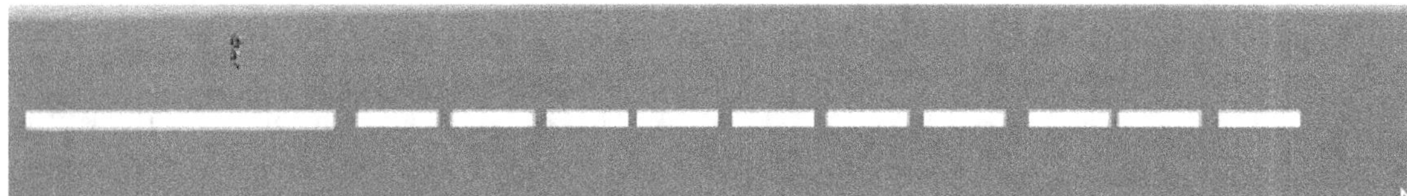

Figure 110: Creating a bridge

- Create an empty object called **shaky_bridge**.

- In the **Hierarchy**, drag and drop all the shaky steps to this empty object so that they become children of this object.

```
▼ shaky_bridge
    shaky_step
    shaky_step (1)
    shaky_step (2)
    shaky_step (3)
    shaky_step (4)
    shaky_step (5)
    shaky_step (6)
    shaky_step (7)
    shaky_step (8)
    shaky_step (9)
```

- You can then drag and drop the object **shaky_bridge** to the **Project** window to create a corresponding prefab.

Last but not least, we will complete this level:

- Please duplicate the long platform and place the duplicate just after the last step (to the right of the scene).

- This will be useful so that you can reuse this level later on if you wish, as part of your game, or simply re-use the prefabs **shaky_step** and **shaky_bridge** to add more challenge to your game.

Please note that, if the steps are very close, they might start to fall, even if the player is not walking on them; this is because of the **Rigidbody2D** component on each of the steps; to avoid this issue, you could, for example, modify the script **ShakyStep**, so that we test first if the collision is with the player (and not with other steps) as follows:

```
void OnCollisionEnter2D (Collision2D coll)
{
        if (coll.gameObject.tag == "Player")
        {
                GetComponent<Rigidbody2D> ().isKinematic = false;
                Destroy (gameObject, 3.0f);
        }
}
```

In this case, you would also need to ensure that the player object has been assigned a tag called **Player**.

INCLUDING LEVEL3 IN THE GAME

As it is, you may notice that **level3** is in isolation, as it is not linked to any of the other levels; so if you'd like it to be accessed through the other levels, you could do the following:

- Add the scene level3 to the **Build Settings**.

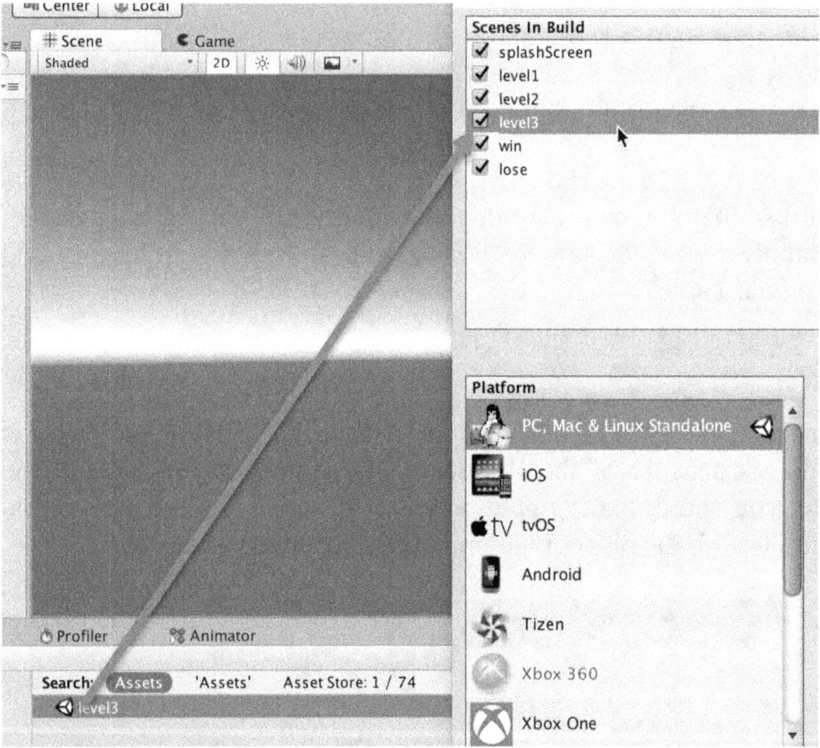

Once this is done, we will need to change the script **DetectCollision**, so that upon completing the second level, the player goes to the **level3** scene;

- Please open the script **DetectCollision**.

- Modify the line that detects the end of level2 as follows (new code in bold).

```
if (tag == "endOfLevel2")
{
    //SceneManager.LoadScene ("win");
    //SceneManager.LoadScene ("level3");
}
```

Once this is done, you can save the script **DetectCollision**. The next step will be to create an object that will symbolize the end of level3 and upon collision with this object, the player will be redirected to the win screen.

- Open the scene **level3**.

- In the project window, look for the object called **endOfLevel2** (i.e., the white square).

- Duplicate this object and call it endOfLevel3.

endOfLevel2
endOfLevel2
endOfLevel3
endOfLevel3

- Drag and drop the asset **endOfLevel3** (i.e., the white square) from the **Project** window to the **Scene** view, towards the end of the level.

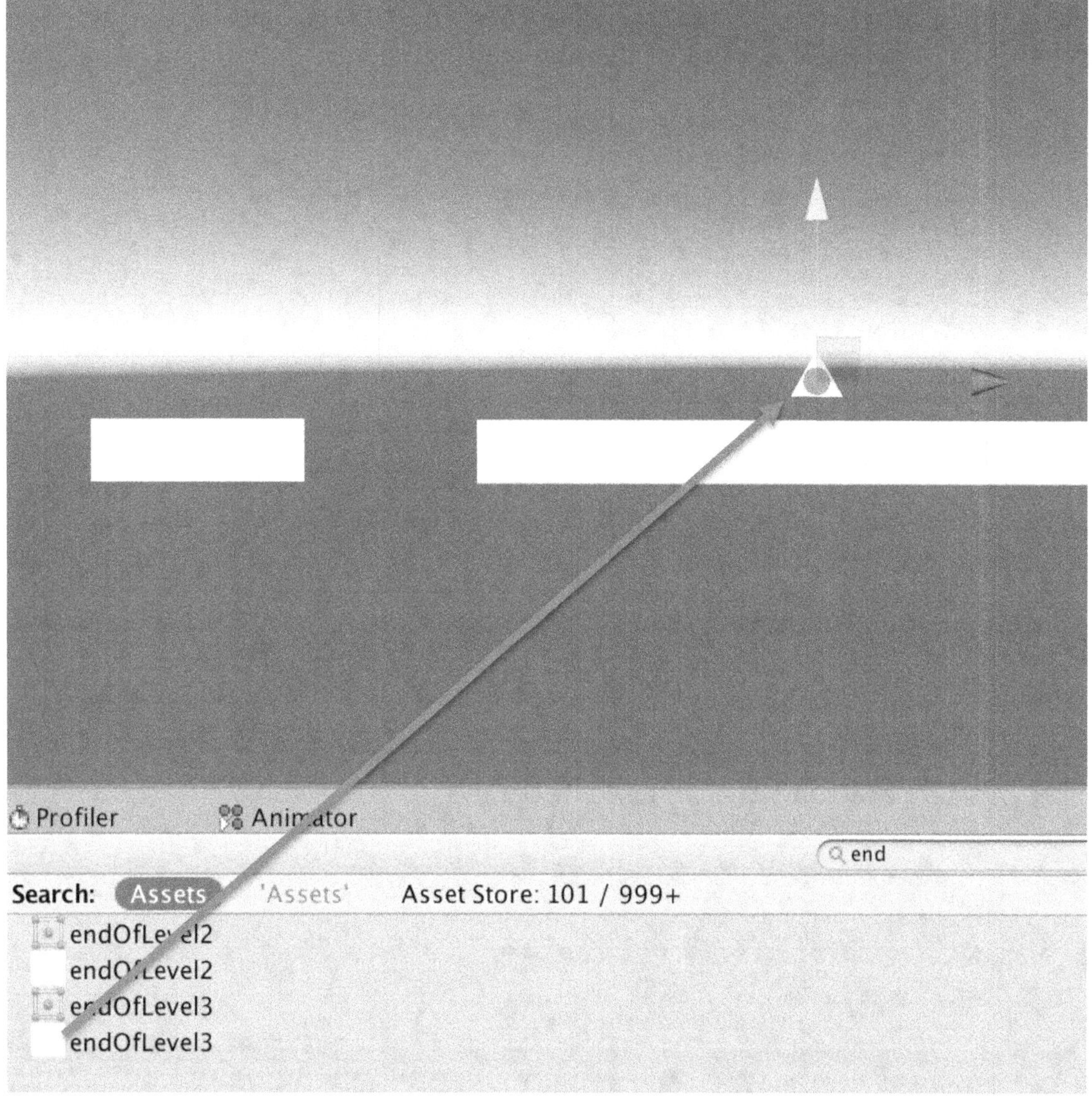

- This will create a new object called **enOfLevel3** in the **Hierarchy** window.

- Add a **Polygon Collider2D** component to this object (**Component | Physics2D | PolygonCollider2D**).

- Create a new tag called **endOfLevel3** and apply this tag to the object **endOflevel3**.

Last but not least, we just need to modify the script **DetectCollision**, so that we can detect when we have reached the end of the third level:

- Please open the script **DetectCollision**.

- Add the following code (new cold in bold).

```
if (tag == "endOfLevel2")
{
     SceneManager.LoadScene ("level3");
}
if (tag == "endOfLevel3")
{
     SceneManager.LoadScene ("win");
}
```

If you want the collection of the coins to be smoother, you could set the objects to collect to triggers, and use the function **OnTriggerEnter2D** in the script **DetectCollision**. In this case, to destroy the object collected from the script you will need to replace this code, in the function **OnTriggerEnter2D**:

```
Destroy (coll.collider.gameObject);
```

With this code:

```
Destroy (coll.GetComponent<CircleCollider2D>().gameObject);
```

If you would like the coins to rotate, you could create a new script attached to each coin (or the prefab called **coin**), with the following code:

```
void Update ()
{
     transform.Rotate (new Vector3(0,1,0));

}
```

In the previous code, we rotate the object around the y-axis every frame.

LEVEL ROUNDUP

In this chapter, we have learned how to improve the game by adding some challenging gameplay components, all stored as prefabs, so that they can be reused in other levels.

Checklist

You can consider moving to the next stage if you can do the following:

- Understand how the option **isKinetic** can be used for **Rigidbody** components.

- Understand how **Time.deltaTime** can be used.

- Understand how to modify the position of an object from a script.

Quiz

Now, let's check your knowledge! Please answer the following questions (the answers are included in the resource pack) or specify whether they are correct or incorrect.

1. An object can be moved from a script using its transform component.

2. **Time.deltaTime** can be used to calculate the delta (difference), in minutes, between two different times.

3. By default, an object with a **Rigidbody2D** component will fall.

4. Using the attribute **isKinematic**, it is possible to ensure that gravity is (temporarily) not applied to an object that includes a **Rigidbody2D** component.

5. To be used as a trigger, an object needs a collider.

6. When an object is used as a trigger, entering its collider will cause the function **OnTriggerEnter2D** to be called.

7. Triggers only apply to square sprites.

8. A scene can be duplicated using the shortcut *CRTL + D*.

9. To copy and paste an object, you can use the shortcut CTRL + D.

10. To update a prefab, you can select an object based on this prefab, select the **Inspector** window, and click the **Apply** button.

Challenge 1

For this chapter, you can improve and expand your existing scenes by adding some of the game mechanics that we have just created; these include:

- Horizontal moving platforms.
- Elevators made of vertical moving platforms.
- Magic doors.
- Shaky bridges.

Challenge 2

You can also try to export your game for the web or as a standalone application:

- Open the **Build Settings**.

- Select the type of export (e.g., Mac/PC/WebGL).

- Click **Build and Run**.

5

FREQUENTLY ASKED QUESTIONS

This chapter provides answers to the most frequently asked questions about the features that we have covered in this book. Please also note that some <u>videos are also available on the companion site</u> to help you with some of the concepts covered in this book.

SCENES

How can I create a scene?

You can create a scene by selecting: **File | New Scene** or by duplicating an existing scene *(CTRL + D)*.

How can I load a new scene from a script?

This scene will need to be added to the **Build Settings** first; then, you can use a code similar to the following to load this scene.

```
Using UnityEngine.UI;
...
...
SceneManager.LoadScene("nameofTheScene");
```

How can I know the name of the current scene from a script?

This can be done by using the following code.

```
SceneManager.GetActiveScene().name;
```

COLLISIONS

What do I need to detect collision?

All objects involved in a collision need to have a **Collider2D** component. Then, you can implement a script that includes the function **OnCollisionEnter2D**.

How do I detect (check the name or the tag of) the object I collided with?

When a collision occurs, the function **OnCollisionEnter2D** will return an object that includes information about the collision; you can use it to access information about the object that you have just collided with, as illustrated in the next code snippet.

```
void OnCollisionEnter2D (Collision2D coll)
{
      string tag = coll.collider.gameObject.tag;
      ...
}
```

What is the difference between a trigger and a collider?

When a collider has been added to a sprite, it can also be set as a trigger; as a collider, it will ensure that the object collides with other objects; in this case, the collision will be detected and processed through the script **OnCollisionEnter2D**; however, in the case of a trigger, this sprite will not collide with other sprites; instead its shape will determine an area that acts as a trigger when entered by another object; in this particular case the function **OntriggerEnter2D** will be called.

How can I make the collection of the coins smoother?

If you want the collection of the coins to be smoother, you could set the objects to collect to triggers, and use the function **OnTriggerEnter2D** in the script **DetectCollision**. This will ensure that the player does not bounce off the objects to be collected, and that they disappear as the player is very close to them (thanks to the trigger).

SAVING DATA OR OBJECTS ACROSS SCENES

What are player preferences?

Player preferences are data that can be stored and access throughout the game as integers, booleans or strings. They can be compared to global variables because their scope (i.e., where they can be used and accessed) is the entire game; so using this concept, data can be saved between scenes.

How do I store or access player preferences?

Player preferences can be accessed and stored easily using a code similar to the following snippet.

```
int score = PlayerPrefs.GetInt("score");//we write information to the player preferences
PlayerPrefs.SetInt("score", 10); //we read information from the player preferences
```

How can I keep objects from being destroyed every-time a new scene is loaded?

You can specify, using the function **Awake**, that the object linked to a particular script should not be destroyed in the next scene; this can be done as follows:

```
void Awake()
{
     DontDestroyOnLoad(transform.gameObject);
}
```

What is the difference between the functions Awake and Start?

The function **Start** is called whenever the script is loaded; so this is usually done at the start of the scene; the function **Awake**, on the other hand, is loaded only once, when the game starts.

SPRITES

Can I create my own sprites in Unity?

Yes, while the 2D assets provided by Unity includes built-in sprites, you can create (and subsequently modify) your own sprites by using the menu **Create | Sprites** from the **Project** window. This makes it possible to create sprites of different shapes including: triangles, circles, or squares. You can also add color to these sprites.

Can I create animated sprites?

Yes, although this is not covered in this book, you can create animated sprites; for this you will need to import several sprites, and then drag and drop the sprites that make-up the animation to the scene view, this will create an animated sprite.

Can I create invisible sprites?

Yes, this can be done by deactivating the **Sprite Renderer** component for a particular sprite.

6
THANK YOU

I would like to thank you for completing this book; I trust that you are now comfortable with creating a simple platform game. This book is the first in the series "Beginner's Guide" that will cover particular aspects of Unity, so it may be time to move on to the next books where you will get started with more specific features such as Virtual reality, 2D shooters, or Character Animation. You can find a description of these forthcoming books on the official page http://www.learntocreategames.com/beginners-guide-to-unity/.

In case you have not seen it yet, you can subscribe to our Facebook group using the following link; it includes a community of like-minded game creators who share ideas and are ready to help you with your game projects.

http://facebook.com/groups/learntocreategames/

You may also subscribe to our mailing list to receive weekly updates and information on how to create games and improve your skills, using the following page:

http://learntocreategames.com/2d-platform-games/

Finally, if you would like to take some of my online video courses, you can head over to learntocreategames.usefedora.com; it includes several courses on Unity 2D and 3D games, with plenty of free tutorials that you can access after a free registration.

So that the book can be constantly improved, I would really appreciate your feedback. So, please leave me a helpful review on Amazon letting me know what you thought of the book and also send me an email (learntocreategames@gmail.com) with any suggestions you may have. I read and reply to every email.

Thanks so much!!